MISSING WOMEN,
MISSING NEWS

MISSING WOMEN, MISSING NEWS

Covering Crisis in Vancouver's Downtown Eastside

David Hugill

Fernwood Publishing • Halifax and Winnipeg

Editing: Jessica Antony
Cover photo: Whitney Davis
Cover design: John van der Woude
Text design: Brenda Conroy
Printed and bound in Canada by Hignell Book Printing

Mixed Sources
Product group from well-managed
forests and other controlled sources
FSC   www.fsc.org Cert no. SW-COC-003438
© 1996 Forest Stewardship Council

Published in Canada by Fernwood Publishing
32 Oceanvista Lane
Black Point, Nova Scotia, B0J 1B0
and 748 Broadway Avenue, Winnipeg, Manitoba, R3G 0X3
www.fernwoodpublishing.ca

Fernwood Publishing Company Limited gratefully acknowledges the financial support of the Government of Canada through the Canada Book Fund, the Canada Council for the Arts, the Nova Scotia Department of Tourism and Culture and the Province of Manitoba, through the Book Publishing Tax Credit, for our publishing program.

Library and Archives Canada Cataloguing in Publication

Hugill, David, 1981-
Missing women, missing news: covering crisis in Vancouver's Downtown Eastside / David Hugill.

(Basics)
Includes bibliographical references.
ISBN 978-1-55266-377-6

1. Missing persons—British Columbia—Vancouver. 2. Murder victims—British Columbia—Vancouver. 3. Prostitutes--British Columbia--Vancouver—Social conditions. 4. Marginality, Social--British Columbia—Vancouver. 5. Pickton, Robert William. 6. Serial murderers—British Columbia. 7. Downtown-Eastside (Vancouver, B.C.). I. Title. II. Series: Basics (Winnipeg, Man.)

HQ150.V3H84 2010   306.74'20971133   C2010-902728-0

Contents

For my old friend Audrey Prier (1918–2009)

"What is an ideology without a space to which it refers, a space which it describes, whose vocabulary and links it makes use of, and whose code it embodies?"

—Henri Lefebvre, The Production of Space

"Once We Became Aware"

Lillian O'Dare was 34 years old when she vanished from the streets of Vancouver's Downtown Eastside. Little is publicly known about her except for a few banal details. Newspaper reports tell us that she shared a birthday with Elvis Presley, had "carefully waved" blond hair and was raised in Williams Lake, but offer little information about who she was, the life she lived or the social and political circumstances that foreground her disappearance (Hawthorn 2007). In contrast to this biographical obscurity, however, her story is freighted with an ominous historical importance. It is marked by the dubious distinction of being the inaugural episode in a pattern of predatory violence that would claim a long list of victims in this district. It was here — in the city's oldest and poorest neighbourhood — that more than sixty local women, many of them street-level sex workers, were murdered or went missing between 1978 and 2002.

In Canada, where rates of violent crime remain comparatively low, murders and abductions can generate significant media attention and mobilize impressive deployments of the resources of law enforcement agencies. The recent disappearance of a Toronto teenager who vanished on her morning commute to school, for example, captivated local and national media for weeks and was the source of a wide-ranging investigation by police (Teotonio 2009). Events like these disrupt widely shared perceptions about what is to be expected in this country. Polling data in recent decades demonstrates that Canadians have a high degree of faith in the capacity of authorities to ensure both their own personal safety and the safety of the population in general (Gannon 2005; Statistics Canada 2005). Violent incidents, in the minds of many, constitute aberrational episodes in a continuum of otherwise orderly co-existence; rare and provocative disruptions of a prevailing peace. When they do occur, it is widely expected that they will be met with a swift and severe response by accountable and professional institutions.

The grisly series of events that unfolded in Vancouver's Downtown Eastside, however, can scarcely be considered aberrational. The disappearance of so many women — sustained over such a significant period — betrays a decidedly different reality; it demonstrates that brutality and predation had become a norm in the neighbourhood. Yet Vancouver's crisis of missing and murdered women generated very little formal interest before 1998, and few outside of the neighbourhood took notice as the crisis was spiraling out of control. O'Dare's disappearance in September of 1978 initiated a trend that would gain momentum rapidly in the years that followed. By the end of the 1980s, for example, an additional ten women had vanished from the neighbourhood. This pace quickened in the early 1990s as roughly a dozen more went missing by 1994. It spiked dramatically again after 1995 and more than thirty new disappearances had occurred by the end of 2001 (Missing Women Task Force 2007). But as the bulk of these crimes had unfolded, local authorities and journalists were missing in action; they made little acknowledgement of the genuine crisis that was taking place. At best, they had failed to notice. At worst, they had failed to care.

So what, then, was different about what happened in Vancouver? Why did the disappearance of a single teenager in Toronto — a tragic but definitively isolated incident — marshal vigorous police and media campaigns while a far more expansive series of tragedies in Vancouver was for a long time met with state inaction and media silence? The answers to these questions are complex and can only begin to be elucidated when we consider how an intersecting series of social and political practices operate to valorize certain lives while simultaneously disregarding others. What's clear is that the social and geographical location of the women that were taken from the Downtown Eastside operated to disqualify them from the protective assurance of authorities. As residents of a stigmatized inner city neighbourhood, sex workers in the bottoms rungs of Vancouver's street-level sex trade, drug users or poverty-stricken members of an increasingly stratified society and as racialized women, they were part of a social segment that was either rendered invisible to, or cast aside from, the core constituencies that are served by our collective institutions. As one politician asked: "do you think if 65 women went missing from Kerrisdale [an affluent Vancouver neighbourhood], we'd have ignored it so long?" (Wood 2004)

Today a rich collection of accounts from friends and allies of the missing and murdered women demonstrate that a prevailing spirit of dismissal defined police approaches to the cases throughout the 1990s. Carrie Kerr, whose sister Helen Hallmark disappeared in this period, recalls that police refused to open a missing persons file. "They told me 'No, go down to the needle exchange and leave her a message there,'" she recalls. Angela Jardine, who asked Vancouver police to follow up on her daughter's disappearance in late 1998, was told not to worry and that her daughter would likely turn up. Police delayed producing a missing persons poster for two months, assuming her disappearance was innocuous (Levitz 2007). Sandra Gagnon, who reported her sister missing in 1997, concedes that she encountered genuinely concerned police officers that were willing to pursue an investigation but was frustrated by their inability to connect individual disappearances to a larger pattern. "They never took the threat seriously... I can guarantee you that if it wasn't the Downtown Eastside, and they weren't hookers, something would have been done in an instant," she says (Amnesty International 2004). Police sustained the view that as "transient" sex workers and drug users, most of the missing had not *actually* disappeared; in most cases, they maintained that the women would soon show up again. They were, of course, devastatingly wrong.

The severity and scope of these events are now well known but their current prominence is deceptive. A recent deluge of bureaucratic, journalistic and political interest in the case contrasts sharply with the prevailing culture of disinterest that had permeated police departments, news rooms and legislative chambers while women were disappearing with a marked frequency for two decades. In contrast to authorities, however, residents of the Downtown Eastside had long been aware that something horrific was unfolding in their midst. Since 1991 local activists have been organizing an annual Valentine's Day march as a public opportunity to honour the victims of violence and demand justice for the disappeared. But in spite of their efforts, few outside the neighbourhood's rugged twenty-one blocks — then as now Canada's "poorest postal code" — bothered to take much notice before a few local journalists began to do some probing.

The first media coverage of the crisis began to trickle out in the summer of 1998. *Vancouver Sun* reporter Lindsay Kines was the first mainstream journalist to catch wind of it. That July, he reported that police had begun to look for connections between ten disappearances of Downtown Eastside women that had been reported since 1996. Anne Drennan, a police liaison officer, assured readers that these files (and an additional six dating back to the late 1980s) were being given "the highest of priorities" (Kines 1998a). Kines' stories generated some initial public pressure. By September, he was reporting that the local force had moved to establish a "working group" to review cases dating back to 1971. As the public profile of the disappearances grew, speculation that they might be the work of a serial killer soon became widespread, but police were careful to play that down (Kines 1998b). By March of the next year, however, police had offered little indication that they were making any headway on the files and public concern had begun to morph into a growing "clamour" (Stall 1999b). Mounting public outrage crystallized in a series of well-attended demonstrations that spring, and local politicians were quickly losing the luxury of indifference. In an effort to demonstrate that they were taking the situation seriously, police officials soon assigned new officers to the investigation (Kines and Culbert 1999). But this alone was insufficient to appease the concerned. Frustrations were exacerbated after police issued two $100,000 rewards for information related to a series of home and garage invasions and allies of the missing women began to ask tough questions about official priorities. As the scale of the disappearances became more broadly known and anxieties about an un-apprehended serial killer built toward a crescendo, the case began to attract outside attention. In the wake of a visit from the television crime program *America's Most Wanted* — in town to do a segment on the disappearances — municipal officials finally acquiesced; in a last-minute effort to mitigate embarrassment, authorities announced that another $100,000 reward would be available to anyone who could provide information leading to an arrest related to the missing women. The initiative, funded and supported by municipal authorities, marked a stark reversal of Mayor Phillip Owen's initial position on the matter. Weeks earlier he had argued that it would be "inappropriate" to use public funds to provide a "location service" for prostitutes (Phillips 1999). When the *America's Most Wanted* segment aired, host John Walsh praised police efforts and spoke approvingly of the reward (Pitman 2002). For many of those who had demanded action, the reward marked an overdue acknowledgement that the crisis was real. The day it was announced, police confirmed the severity of the situation; Drennan told reporters: "Once we became aware… that there was clearly something wrong here, something that we should be concerned about, we started to kick in additional resources" (Cameron 2007). But a well-documented record contradicts police claims. It is now clear that no such vigorous pursuit of answers had transpired *as soon as* police became aware that women were disappearing. In contrast, police and municipal authorities had displayed a chronic lack of interest as the case had spiraled catastrophically out of control.

Little hard evidence had been gathered by the fall of 2000 and the police department announced that they would scale back the review team that had been established. But even as police attention ebbed, the number of disappeared continued to mount: seventeen women went missing between 1999 and 2001. Concerned with the lack of progress, Kines and other *Sun* reporters launched a four-month investigation of the cases in 2001 and unveiled a damning series of revelations. They determined, among other things, that the official police figure of twenty-seven missing women was woefully inadequate and that at least forty-five cases should have been part of the investigation. They also concluded that while police had taken pains to maintain the appearance of an "aggressive, concerned investigation," their work had been devastatingly tainted by petty in-fighting, the absence of coherent leadership and a distinct lack of resources (*Vancouver Sun* 2002). It was now clear that, in spite of their protestations to the contrary, police could hardly claim to have made the investigation a real priority. Once again confronted with a spiraling public relations disaster — and an ever-expanding roster of missing women — Vancouver police were forced to take new action. Weeks later, they joined forces with the Royal Canadian Mounted Police to form the inter-jurisdictional Missing Women Joint Task Force.

The new unit raided a farm in suburban Port Coquitlam one year later. It soon became clear that the search was related to the missing women and the investigation quickly took on a robust media profile. Local and national media were captivated by speculation that Robert Pickton — one of the farm's owners who had been detained on a series of weapons charges — was being considered as a person of interest in the case. Pickton was well known in the area; he and his brother David operated a registered charity organization called Piggy Palace Good Times Society that was known for the large-scale parties and events it held on the farm. In the weeks that followed, journalistic digging and information that trickled out from investigators suggested that these events were often boisterous affairs that frequently included sex workers from the Downtown Eastside, often lured to the property with the promise of money and drugs. As early details became available, journalists anticipated that the dramatic prosecution of a serial killer would soon unfold and the story quickly soared to the top of news agendas.

Two weeks later, police confirmed media speculation and Pickton was charged with murdering two of the missing women. Within a year, ten additional murder charges were added to the indictment against him. By 2005, that number would climb to twenty-seven. If convicted, Pickton would become Canada's most prolific serial killer. Not surprisingly, media interest matched the magnitude of the accusations and the story generated prominent coverage for months.

That same interest would return again with a pronounced vigour in January 2007 when the trial phase of the proceedings against Pickton opened in New Westminster, British Columbia. The original indictment had been split in two during the *voir-dire* hearings and the Crown was instructed to proceed initially with six charges of first-degree murder. The lessened ambitions of the court did not dissuade the media, however, and a swarm of nearly four hundred media workers descended on the suburban courtroom to cover the story (Cameron 2007). It was a short-lived assignment for most; they were there to provide an initial context and then move on, not to return again until a verdict had been reached. For the Canadian print media, however, the trial seemed to merit a more thorough examination. Correspondents were enlisted to follow the minutia of trial developments but also to put the story in a larger socio-political context. In fact, this work had already begun for many newspapers. Since the initial raid of the Pickton farm nearly five years earlier, they had run stories that attempted to look beyond the particular *modus operandi* of the accused and examine what else could help to explain how dozens of women could be made to disappear from a densely populated urban neighbourhood. Many reporters looked to the Downtown Eastside for answers. Lurid portrayals suggested that the neighbourhood's "mean streets" and the social status of people on society's "fringes" offered part of the answer. Police negligence and bureaucratic inefficiency seemed to offer another. These early reports demonstrated that the case was bigger than being about a deranged killer; it was also about a criminal underworld, a dangerous part of town, rapacious addictions, damaged and vulnerable individuals and indifferent or incompetent authorities. Local and national audiences would be exposed to an expansive consideration of these dimensions by the time the case had concluded.

This book considers how the national print media told the story of Vancouver's missing and murdered women through their coverage of the proceedings against Robert Pickton. I want to stress, at the outset, that this coverage was neither monolithic nor uncomplicated. It is important to acknowledge that it was laudably expansive in a number of ways. Members of the press were instrumental, for example, in demonstrating that a simple consideration of the serial killer himself was entirely inadequate to explain what had happened in the Downtown Eastside. In sum, they provided a coherent framework for understanding the tragedy, a compelling series of dominant narratives through which audiences might make sense of what happened in Vancouver. But these prevailing explanations, thorough as they may be, provoke a number of questions. Is a consideration of irresponsible policing, for example, sufficient to explain the state's complicity in the crisis? Do sympathetic portrayals of the victims disrupt the relentless stigmatization and demonization of street-involved women? Are audiences given enough information about the Downtown Eastside to adequately assess why social suffering and violence seem to have become so concentrated in this district?

This book is primarily an attempt to answer these questions. In what follows, I demonstrate that the dominant themes that emerge from the coverage provide a series of explanations that insufficiently examine the range of instruments and assumptions that operated to imperil the women that disappeared from the Downtown Eastside. I argue that the coverage effectively reduces the case to a series of contingencies — albeit an expansive list of them — that camouflage the functioning of structural and cultural systems of domination. That is, they offer a series of coherent explanations that hold particular individuals and practices accountable but largely omit, conceal or erase altogether the broader socio-political context that rendered those practices possible.

The Canadian Mediascape

My observations are based on case-related materials extracted from the Ontario editions of three of Canada's principal English-language daily newspapers, the *Toronto Star*, the *Globe and Mail* and the *National Post*. They are drawn from three periods of heightened interest in the case: the first begins with the raid on the Pickton farm and ends shortly after he was charged with the initial counts of first-degree murder (February 8–27, 2002); the second encompasses the opening week of the trial and the days that immediately preceded it (January 20–27, 2007); and the third encompasses the conclusion of the trial and the sentencing of the convicted (December 1–12, 2007). A group of 157 articles and a large number of corresponding images and photographs constitute these case-related materials. I treat these articles as an aggregate product in an effort to give a broad impression of how the story was told by the national print media. But I do this cautiously and with full knowledge that the messages they contain are interpreted by audiences in a wide variety of ways. News discourses are instruments of knowledge production, to be sure, but that knowledge is processed and reconstituted in ways at least as diverse as the audiences that absorb it.

I examine these particular newspapers for a number of reasons. First, all three are non-Vancouver based and their correspondents could not assume that audiences would be acquainted with the case. The crisis had been extensively considered for years in local newspapers but these outside sources were all relative newcomers when the story acquired a national profile in 2002. Each needed to establish the broader context of the case for its audience. This necessity determined a certain consistency between the news rhythms of each source that allowed me to compare them coherently. I also focus on these newspapers because each reaches (and presumably influences) a broad readership. They are the three most circulated English-language dailies in the country, as table 0.1 demonstrates. The *National Post* and the *Globe and Mail* are the country's only national dailies while the *Toronto Star* is produced and distributed in the country's most densely populated region. Finally, other dailies tend to rely on wire services and press agencies for much of what they publish while these papers produce the majority of their content internally; they serve a generative rather than reproductive function within their parent corporations and news narratives produced by these papers often re-circulate through other outlets. This is particularly notable given the sprawling range of media outlets held by each source's ownership group. Bell Globemedia (owner of the *Globe and Mail*), CanWest Global (owner of the *National Post*) and the Torstar Corporation (owner of the *Toronto Star*), collectively produce nearly half of the newspapers circulated each day in this country, as table 0.2 demonstrates.

Recent research demonstrates that Canadians now rely on a broad diversity of sources for information about current affairs so it is necessary to explain why this study focuses exclusively on newspaper narratives (Hermida 2008). This is particularly important since the former leaders of news dissemination, the nightly network television news and the daily newspaper, have seen their influence wane in recent years as a wide proliferation of web-based and specialty channel sources have eroded their dominance. Despite these trends, however, both have retained a significant stake in mass media markets. Television remains by far the most relied upon source with more than 65 percent of poll respondents reporting that they consult it regularly (Standing Senate Committee on Transport and Communications [hereafter SSCTC] 2006). Daily newspapers continue to lag significantly behind their televisual counterparts but they do remain the second most consumed medium with slightly less than 20 percent of respondents reporting regular consultation.

Table 0.1 English-Language Canadian Newspapers, by Circulation (2007)

Newspaper	Average Daily Circulation	Percentage of Total Daily Newspaper Circulation (Canada)
Toronto Star	465,803	9.9
Globe and Mail	337, 387	7.2
National Post	206,003	4.4
Toronto Sun	194,042	4.1
Vancouver Sun	171,782	3.6
Total	1,009,193 (top three)	21.58 (top three)

Source: Canadian Newspaper Association 2008.

Table 0.2 Average Daily Circulation, by Ownership Group (2007)

Newspaper	Average Daily Circulation	Percentage of Total Daily Newspaper Circulation (Canada)
CanWest (*National Post*)	1,163,886	24.8
Torstar Corporation (*Toronto Star*)	654,164	13.9
Bell GlobeMedia (*Globe and Mail*)	337,387	7.2
Total	2,155,437	45.9

Source: Canadian Newspaper Association 2008.

They are most often read by Canadians aged 45–64, a powerful and influential demographic. Moreover, newspapers in general, and these three in particular, remain key sources of information for both business and political elites. There is also significant evidence that newspapers continue to propel the agendas of other media, particularly television news (Soderlund and Hildebrandt 2005). This is of particular note in a case like this one, where particular political practices are held up to scrutiny. Further, newspapers have retained a significant edge on radio and magazine sources in all demographics and an edge on Internet sources in most (sscтc 2006). Yet in spite of these successes, newspapers no longer enjoy the consumer loyalty that once seemed inevitable. Research that considers the political importance of newspaper messages must account for this decline. It cannot simply be assumed that print narratives are representative of *media opinion* generally; they must be understood as one group of articulations in an ever-expanding field.

On the surface, the diversification of media sources would seem to signal a correlative diversification of media opinion. But while technological advance has afforded alternative news sources an unprecedented capacity to reach audiences, recent trends in media ownership suggest that the diversity of news narratives is contracting. The vast majority of widely consulted media outlets are now owned by a small number of corporate conglomerates. This trend has been particularly pronounced in the Canadian newspaper industry and in some urban centres it has resulted in a near or total monopoly of newspaper ownership (sscтc 2006). CanWest, for example, has achieved total saturation in Regina, Saskatoon and Vancouver, where the corporation controls all of the city's dailies and total linguistic saturation in Montreal where they control all of the English-language dailies (Soderlund and Hildebrandt 2005).

Yet concentrated media ownership is not exclusively a print phenomenon and most of the major newspaper-holding conglomerates own other media outlets too.

Table O.3 Urban Market Share, by Ownership Group

Market	Ownership Group	Market Share of Television Newscasts (%)	Market Share of Daily Newspapers (%)
Vancouver	CanWest	70.6	100.0
Edmonton	CanWest	39.7	60.0
Quebec City	Quebecor	47.1	56.2
Toronto	Bell GlobeMedia	43.8	18.3
	CanWest	33.0	11.5
Regina	CanWest	28.3	100.0
Montreal (English)	CanWest	5.0	100.0
Montreal (French)	Quebecor	37.1	60.4

Source: Soderlund and Hildebrandt 2005.

CanWest's sprawling corporate empire marks an extreme but not unique example of this trend. In addition to a wide diversity of local and national newspapers, the corporation now controls a major national television broadcaster with dozens of local broadcast affiliates, a host of specialty cable channels, a series of high profile, web-based news sources, radio stations, magazines and other key communications assets. Though less pronounced, this trend is repeated with other media conglomerates, including Bell GlobeMedia and Torstar. These few conglomerates wield a decisive influence in local and national mediascapes and have an unrivalled capacity to define both how the news is presented and what counts as news at all.

There are few considerations of these questions of ownership, consolidation and convergence in what follows. My analysis is focused on the content of media messages and pays scarce attention to the corporate environment in which they are incubated and shaped. In spite of this absence, I remain convinced that the corporate structure of media production is central to a full consideration of the content of media messages.

Ideology as the Reproduction of Commonsense

The assertion that the coverage privileges a series of *dominant* narratives that mislead or deceive, as I suggest above, must be considered in some detail. It is not sufficient to suggest — without qualification — that these mystifications simply *appear* in news narratives. In fact, the contention that deception occurs at all begs a number of important questions. Are the press implicated in a grand conspiracy to conceal the *true* nature of this crisis? Are individual journalists beholden to a certain constellation of power and therefore compelled to distort? Do structural limits or editorial expectations somehow restrict a full telling of the story of the missing and murdered women? My own view is that a strictly conspiratorial analysis of the mass media — one that suggests individual journalists knowingly and actively deceive — is simply untenable. Nevertheless, as the analysis that follows will demonstrate, there are jarring disconnections between the explanations of the crisis that are privileged by the coverage and a well-established historical record which seems to contradict them. But if journalists are not in the business of deliberate manipulation, how can we account for these disparities?

In what follows, I adopt a particular conception of ideology as a way to approach this question. But this approach is not without its dangers: the terrain of ideology is fraught with contestation. The term has not only been frequently rejected by its opponents as an overly-reductionist way to understand complex social relations, but there is also no coherent agreement amongst its adherents about what constitutes an ideology. Ideology has also been employed divergently by a wide range of intellectual traditions; as Terry Eagleton (1991: 1) points out, the term itself is "woven of a whole tissue of different conceptual strands." Thus at the outset — and in the interest of theoretical precision — it is important to outline precisely what is meant when I invoke the term ideology in this volume.

I theorize ideology not as a static or abstract set of propositions but as a series of representational and discursive practices that are embedded in commonsense or taken-for-granted assumptions about what our society is and how it works (Hall 1981). This book considers how press reports operate to reproduce such assumptions by establishing particular "frameworks" through which audiences are given the opportunity to make sense of the crisis of missing and murdered women. Ideology, in this sense, is not simply an aggregation of the political preferences or beliefs of individuals but a broad analytical space — a "field of power," to borrow a phrase from Pierre Bourdieu — in which members of a society tend to formulate understandings of the world that they inhabit (Hackett and Carroll 2006). I share the view that our individual positions of identification are frequently constructed within the boundaries of such fields. Put differently, my inquiry begins from the premise that "ideologies are not really produced by individual consciousness but rather individuals formulate their beliefs ... within positions already fixed by ideology" (Larrain 1996: 49). I am, of course, cognizant of Michel Foucault's (1980) warning about the inadequacy of theoretical work that seeks to explain domination through an all-determining "infrastructure," a gesture which risks collapsing the wide proliferation of power relations into a single set of discrete knowable forms. Connectedly, I share Jean-Francois Lyotard's (1984) suspicions about the danger of relying on a single coherent narrative to explain the diversity of social phenomena that are at play in a given milieu. Nevertheless, I remain committed to the view that a theory of ideology offers an effective way to confront the pronounced contradictions inherent in press representations of the crisis. I accept the contention that, in some sense, all discourses are *ideological* in that all discourses are both partial and subjective. Nevertheless, my concern here is with those discourses that — by virtue of this partiality — provide definitions that support and sustain an established constellation of power or particular modes of domination. I insist on the term ideology because it is precisely this relationship that I want to elucidate in this book.

In the analysis that follows, I will argue that a prevailing ideological logic was not only central to the production of the very possibility of the crisis but also at the core of the dominant news discourse mobilized to explain it. I agree with Jennifer England (2004: 296), who argues that "although the boundary between discourse and everyday life is fluid, complex, and often disrupted, it is important to trace these connections, particularly when discrimination and oppression are at work." Thus at the core of my analysis is a prevailing interest in unmasking the material dispossession that particular discursive constructions conceal. I pursue these erasures and obfuscations "without guarantees" and make no claim to scientific certainty (Hall 1996).

Ideology and News Discourses

Mass media institutions have access to striking concentrations of symbolic power. As such, they exist in a decisively ideological sphere; they are key sites where social meanings are produced and distributed (Hall 1981). Thus not surprisingly, communication researchers have long been interested in the relationship between mass media messages and social and political power. Stuart Hall et al. (1978: 65), in their seminal consideration of a perceived mugging outbreak in the United Kingdom, consider why news narratives have tended to "reproduce and sustain... definitions of... situation[s] which favour the powerful." Thirty years later, the premise of their inquiry is hardly controversial; a wide diversity of scholarship has been dedicated to answering precisely this question and a number of compelling schools of thought have been mobilized and developed to do so.

In light of now well-established suspicions about the effects of media practices, it is easy to forget that some media scholars once considered (and, in some cases, continue to consider) mass media institutions as the exemplars of an engaged democratic citizenship. Mass media scholarship was once dominated by a series of liberal-pluralist assumptions that presented the institution of journalism as a "watchdog against the abuse of power, a righter of wrongs, a humbler of hubris and arrogance, a promoter of positive social change, [and] an agent to comfort the afflicted and afflict the comfortable" (Hackett and Carroll 2006: 21). In the first half of the twentieth century, celebrated research saw the potential of mass media communication as inherently democratic. Social behaviorists like George Mead (1948: 326) argued that the proliferation of instruments of mass communication would provide a basis for social unity by providing individuals with the means to "identify themselves with each other." These approving assessments of the press were often sustained and reproduced by what media institutions said (and continue to say) about themselves. David Taras (1990), for example, suggests that the "mirror model" — which holds that mass media news discourses mirror reality and reflect issues and events as they truly are — is "widely accepted" among individuals working within news-generating organizations. Geneva Overholser and Kathleen Jamieson (2005) suggest that notions of media "mirroring" are still common among news institutions and animate professional pretensions of objectivity. Yet others have challenged this paradigm, suggesting that news discourses do not simply reflect reality but act as active agents of representation that hold up a "distorted mirror" which alters fundamentally the content it reflects (Taras 1990).

More prominently, a wide diversity of scholars have argued that the relationship between media outputs and political power hinges crucially on questions of ownership. Researchers have argued that the status of news-generating organizations as privately-owned corporations has engendered a near-seamless relationship between media messages and the interests of capital. Noam Chomsky and Edward Herman (1988) famously proposed that a "propaganda model" could be used to evaluate the extent of this relationship. They claimed that media messages must be evaluated according to the five "filters" through which they must pass before being deemed fit for publication or broadcast. In this schema, the outputs of corporate media institutions will tend to reflect the interests of its owners, advertisers and those who fund its activities, as well as the opinions of those who are deemed appropriate sources and able to provide information quickly (well-financed and organized government and private institutions, including the military, for example). Media messages, they contend, are also tempered by the need to avoid flak from centres of power and by the prevailing ideologies of a society's most powerful interests (for Chomsky and Herman this included the "national religion of anti-communism"). Consistently, Michael Parenti (1993: 51) maintains that corporate ownership has had a decisive impact on media outputs. He argues that because corporate power permeates the "entire social fabric" of our societies, "opinions that support existing arrangements of economic and political power are more easily treated as facts." Prevailing notions of objectivity, therefore, necessarily reflect these particular biases and much of "what is reported as 'news' is little more than the uncritical transmission of official opinions."

Yet others have argued that while questions of ownership are instructive, a thorough analysis of the relationship between media messages and established power must consider the relative autonomy of individual journalists. Hall et al. (1978) stress that news messages are themselves a social product and insist that understanding their relationship to power requires understanding the "professional ideology" in which they are incubated and deployed. To this end, they examine the professional practices that shape news discourses, pointing to a series of structural necessities that influence news production to explain why media institutions tend to provide an "over-accessing" to people and institutions in positions of power. But perhaps more centrally for our present purposes, they also argue that media messages are articulated within "distinct ideological limits" and thus necessarily provide "frameworks" for evaluating issues that tend to tip in favour of established authority. Similarly, Ericson et al.'s (1991: 3–4) sprawling survey of media practices found that news discourses serve an inherently conservative function in that they perpetually "represent order" by installing particular views of "morality, procedural form, and social hierarchy" that promote particular "versions and visions" of social control. Nevertheless, they argue that the contention that news reproduces ideologies that are in "favour of the powerful" is too simplistic. They suggest that because the effects of media messages "vary substantially," conclusions about their particular impacts are often too presumptive (Ericson et al. 1991: 19). Todd Gitlin (2001: 141) echoes this sentiment. He warns against the view that "media imprints are uniformly potent," a dangerous assumption, in his estimation, which can quickly lead the critic to "collapse the whole of life into a shadow projected by the garish light of the media, a dumb show played out on the wall's of Plato's cave." Yet others still, especially Bourdieu (1993), stress the importance of recognizing that power is dispersed in particular and often autonomous "fields" that are situated in a broader constellation of political possibility. Hackett and Carroll (2006: 48) summarize this approach's applicability to the mass media, suggesting that it "invites us to consider journalism and mass media as relatively autonomous fields within a broader field of power, which is itself structured in dominance."

My own theoretical approach is informed by a number of these positions. First, while I want to distance myself from a conspiratorial view of the media, I also want to stress that the newspapers I examine are owned by corporate conglomerates with an undeniable set of interests. Nevertheless, I hold that many of the problematic messages that the coverage reproduces have more to do with the "professional ideology" of news production than with the structure of their ownership (Hall et al. 1978). Ultimately, though, I agree with Hackett and Carroll (2006: 33) that "the media are powerful in so far as they comprise a concentration of society's symbolic power." Following Bourdieu, I think it is useful to consider particular media institutions as somewhat autonomous but stress that the opinions they produce are primarily shaped by the prevailing frameworks which are themselves the products of a broader "field" of dominant power.

Ideology and the Case of the Missing and Murdered Women

My analysis is primarily concerned with a consideration of the newspaper coverage's concealment of certain dimensions of the case of the missing and murdered women, as I note above. Slavoj Zizek (1994: 4) argues that the task of the "critique of ideology is to discern the hidden necessity in what appears to be mere contingency." In many ways, the present project is engaged in such a critique. In the chapters that follow I demonstrate how particular explanations of the crisis have operated to conceal, minimize or deny the "hidden necessity" inherent in the functioning of particular systems of domination, even if such explanations do not reduce the crisis to mere contingency.

My observations are indebted to a number of other studies that have considered media representation of the missing and murdered women and have attempted to reveal a certain "hidden logic" of domination. Yasmin Jiwani and Mary-Lynn Young's (2006: 902) survey of case-related articles that appeared in the *Vancouver Sun* between 2001 and 2006, for example, argues that a reproduction of historically entrenched (and contemporarily prevailing) stereotypes about street-involved women, Aboriginality and more generally the sex trade has had the effect of "demarcat[ing] the boundaries of respectability and degeneracy" and reproducing particular kinds of marginality. Their analysis observes that journalists employed a "moral and racialized economy of representations" to describe the disappeared women. They observe that

> within this economy, racialized status, such as Aboriginality, interlocks with prostitution to position these women in the lower echelon of a moral order… [and] the stereotypical attributes ascribed to both of these positions feed into and reproduce common-sense notions of itinerant and irresponsible behavior, which is then seen as naturally inviting victimization. (Jiwani and Young 2006: 902)

Dara Culhane's (2003: 595) considerations of the crisis suggest that a similar journalistic logic has operated to conceal particular women (primarily Aboriginal women) behind a "regime of disappearance" — a pattern of knowledge production that "selectively marginalizes and/or erases categories of people through strategies of representation that include silences, blind spots, and displacements that have both material and symbolic effects." England (2004: 300) echoes these sentiments and suggests that representations of the missing women have rendered them simultaneously invisible (in Culhane's sense) and hyper-visible; she suggests that they are at once "inside and outside the gaze of the state." My own project has much in common with these other studies and I draw on them repeatedly in the analysis that follows. Perhaps the central theoretical departure of my own study, however, is an insistence on the use of the term *ideology* to describe the ways in which these *logics* of domination function.

Reconsidering Dominant Explanations

This book attempts to supplement and counter the partial explanations that emerge from the coverage in four core arguments. Each one highlights a particular erasure or mystification.

The first demonstrates that the coverage's focus on police negligence provides a compelling way to understand how more than sixty women could disappear. I argue that considerations of incompetent or unconcerned policing offer a compelling way to understand the lack of an official response as the list of missing women continued to swell. But by overemphasizing this explanation, I contend, the state's role in the tragedy is limited to a series of personal or bureaucratic failures and broader considerations of state culpability are effectively minimized.

The second argument demonstrates how the state itself was directly complicit in the tragedy in at least three ways. I argue that the retrenchment of state systems of social solidarity, the ongoing effects of colonialism, and the criminal regulation of prostitution, were (and continue to be) central to the marginalization and endangerment of certain women. While these particular modes of subordination are considered in the press coverage, they are done so in ways that minimize their foundational complicity in the crisis.

The third argument demonstrates how this minimization is accomplished through narratives that purport to explain the lives and motivations of street-involved women. I consider how certain portrayals establish street-level sex workers as morally and socially distinct from other women. I contend that descriptions that establish women as damaged and deranged operate to make their presence in the dangerous world of the inner city understandable, an important discursive move that helps to explain and rationalize their victimization.

The final argument demonstrates how the Downtown Eastside itself is produced as a space of chaos and criminality. I show how such portrayals present the area as a dangerous and detestable zone, a marginal space where violence and criminality are to be expected. Here, I challenge the suggestion that the neighbourhood's problems can be explained by the presence of a criminal element. I counter such contentions by demonstrating how particular economic and political patterns have operated to isolate the Downtown Eastside from other city spaces and to concentrate particular kinds of social phenomena there.

The common thread that courses through each of these arguments is an attempt to reveal that the explanations provided by the coverage are inadequate, misguided or incomplete. This book attempts to supplement these definitions by expanding the field of who and what might be considered complicit in the production of the intersectional forms of marginalization and dispossession that give this tragedy its particular form.

Chapter 1

Defining the Boundaries of the Crisis

V ancouver's crisis of missing and murdered women presents a potent challenge
to liberal-pluralist claims about the essential fairness of governance in Canada.
The absence of a dramatic official response as scores of women disappeared for
two decades from a densely populated urban neighbourhood demonstrates the
profound contradiction of the state's supposed capacity to provide a basic level of
universal protection. It jars against widely-held views that Canada is a "humanistic, tolerant, and accommodating society" (Henry and Tator 2002: 228). More
precisely, the crisis provides compelling evidence of the selectivity of the Charter-
enshrined guarantee of individual "security of the person."[1] It demonstrates that
the protective and restrictive capacities of police and other authorities are not
dispensed with blind universality but rather meted out with sharp particularity.
Fully considered, the crisis is about much more than the psychopathic caprices
of a serial killer; it reveals how a particular group of marginalized women were
disqualified from the protective assurances of the state.

The media storm generated by the arrest and trial of Robert Pickton offered
a rare opportunity for these divisions to be considered publicly. As the story
developed and reports of unresponsive policing, bureaucratic bungling and the
cold dismissal of a population assumed to be transient became part of the story's
larger narrative, such a consideration seemed a genuine possibility. As the depths
of official negligence became known, the legitimacy of certain state institutions and
actors was indeed called into question (Pitman 2002). Yet despite the willingness of
many journalists to criticize official failure — in some cases installing it as a central
theme in their explanations — the news discourses on which these observations
are based have had the paradoxical effect of actually camouflaging the state's role
in the tragedy. By privileging the negligence of local authorities — what I will call
the negligence narrative — they have operated to mask much larger contradictions
of the state's claim to protect and restrict without distinction. In so doing, they
serve to legitimate the prevailing political order by defining the boundaries of the
crisis in ways that erase or minimize the state's implication in the violence.

Liberal Assumptions and News Narratives

In liberal societies like Canada, the authority of the state is said to be rooted in
a social contract that establishes that all citizens are entitled to certain rights and
assurances and are subject to certain restrictions. In contrast to the state that rules

by coercion, the liberal notion of government by consent establishes the state as a representative authority. It is mandated to ensure a common peace through the maintenance of institutions that mediate conflict, address contradictions and afford certain guarantees universally. The state's monopoly on the legitimate use of violence — the power to police and incarcerate, for example — stems from the larger imperative of maintaining a prevailing sense of order (Hall et al. 1978).

However, such authority is not merely given; it is sustained through demonstrations of the state's fundamental adherence to certain normative standards. The legitimacy of liberal power is contingent on the ability of authorities to make persuasive claims, "arguments that they are acting in accordance with social norms" (Ericson et al. 1991: 7). State power is justified through demonstrations of commitment to established procedures and actions that communicate congruence between the decisions of officials and determined standards of what constitutes an acceptable exercise of power. Where authority is premised on the presumption of a consensus, those who hold power must demonstrate their commitment to certain core universalizing practices, including the maintenance of institutions that ensure that the public expectation of particular forms of equality are met. Legal institutions are vital to this legitimating process; the enforcement of laws grounds the authority of the state in normative practices (Ericson et al. 1991). The policing of crime, for example, derives legitimacy from the perception that it adheres to an established universal standard, the Criminal Code. The enforcement of such norms operates to justify authority by making it appear natural. Institutions that fail to demonstrate a commitment to these norms risk a potential challenge to their legitimacy. If police are thought to be violating public expectations — if their actions are seen as inappropriate or corrupt, for example — then public consent for their authority may be called into question.

News narratives play a vital role in representing and maintaining this prevailing order. Media institutions have the ability to establish the "boundaries of public discourse," and it is within these boundaries that "priorities are set and public agendas are established" (Henry and Tator 2002: 235). Ericson et al. (1991) suggest that such narratives are important sites for state actors and institutions to win legitimacy for their political preferences by establishing their practices within broader definitions of order. As they put it:

> The news-media institution is pivotal to the ability of authorities to make convincing claims. It offers a pervasive and persuasive means by which authorities from various institutions can attempt to obtain wider consent for their moral preferences. Moral authority is always subject to *consent*, and legitimacy is always something that is *granted*. [emphasis in original]

News discourses constitute a distinct site of social struggle where claims and counter-claims compete to define the analytic boundaries of a given event or issue (Hall 1981).

Some contend that such contestations disproportionately benefit established authority and work to reproduce the legitimacy of the prevailing political order (Hall et al. 1978). To take such a position, however, is not necessarily to take a strictly conspiratorial view of the media as a set of institutions that intentionally persuade and manipulate in the service of power. More nuanced analyses have suggested that the structural tendency to reproduce "order" (and the state as its legitimate broker) has more to do with established journalistic practices which rely on certain "taken-for-granted value commitments and reality judgments" which are naturalized and transformed into common sense (Hackett and Carroll 2006: 31). Hall et al. (1978: 54–56) stress the importance of attending to the ways in which news stories are almost always articulated within pre-existing ideological structures which "form the basis of our cultural knowledge," a process that frequently reproduces "crucial assumptions about what society is and how it works." One such assumption is the "consensual nature" of modern liberal democratic societies. They contend that conventional journalistic processes both "assume" and "construct" such a consensus by offering modes of understanding that reflect the view that "we have fundamental interests, values and concerns in common." News narratives that already assume a prevailing consensus carry with them a series of profound political implications. Such views, they propose, operate to deny or minimize real differences between groups; they mask the ways our formal institutions effect peoples' lives in very different ways. These structural discrepancies are concealed by the reproduction of the view that legitimate institutional structures exist to mediate contradictions and provide certain guarantees in a universal way. For Hall et al. (1978: 54–56) such narrations include the assumptions that political institutions guarantee a base-level equality of access in formal decision-making processes, that economic structures allow individuals to have "a stake in the making and distribution of wealth" and that the law operates to protect and restrict in a consistent way. They offer explanations of events, in short, that legitimate the prevailing political order by suggesting and assuming that society operates from a "framework of agreement."

The coverage of the proceedings against Robert Pickton provides an explanation of the crisis of missing and murdered women that reproduces core assumptions about the consensual nature of Canadian society. In its effects (if not in its intention), such narrations operate to manage the crisis by providing compelling *ways of seeing* that occlude broader questions about the legitimacy of the prevailing political order itself and its liberal claims to egalitarian representation.

Defining the Crisis: The Negligence Narrative

For media audiences in Vancouver, the view that police failure was complicit in the tragedy of missing and murdered women was already well established when authorities began their excavation of the Pickton farm in 2002. As Beverly Pitman

(2002) observes, accusations that both the mayor and the police had bungled the cases began to emerge with the first local coverage of the disappearances in 1998 and 1999. She argues that a narrative of negligence — though secondary to other explanations — became part of the "media mill" for three reasons. First, it aligned with the stigmatization of the Downtown Eastside as a centre of criminality and vice, which had been privileged in dominant media discourses for nearly two decades. Second, friends and supporters of the missing women managed to make the case that the police operated on a double-standard and had avoided instigating a full investigation because the victims worked in the street-level sex trade. Third, for a brief period, the "representational work" of supporters, activists and sympathetic journalists had managed to generate an outpouring of sympathy that transcended well-established divisions between the Downtown Eastside and other parts of the city. And while Pitman (2002: 175–76) observes that this "uncommon kind of community" was eventually eroded by the inscription of fears that a serial killer was at work — the installation of a "Jack the Ripper" template — it is nevertheless important to acknowledge that these criticisms of police mismanagement did play a role in early local coverage. Jiwani and Young (2006) make similar observations in their survey of case-related content that appeared in the *Vancouver Sun*. They note that police negligence was sustained as a core element of these narratives but was profoundly overshadowed by a shift in media focus toward Pickton himself.

Outside of British Columbia, however, the tragedy of Vancouver's missing and murdered women did not become a major news story until authorities began to search the Pickton farm in February 2002. As the case developed a truly national profile, considerations of police negligence became an important part of its narration. In fact, within forty-eight hours of the initial raid, police negligence had been established as a central theme in the coverage of all three news sources. Appearing beneath headlines like "Police slow to accept crime link," "B.C. police lashed over probe," "Response by police under fire" and "Police told about farm many times," these early stories inaugurated a period of incisive police criticism.

From February 8 to 22, 2002, nearly one third of all articles related to the case dealt directly with the failure of law enforcement. Friends and supporters of the missing women were central to this critique; their frequently quoted accounts of disinterested investigators, ignored information and a prevailing culture of unwillingness to take disappearances seriously established official negligence as a definitive explanation. Such claims were powerfully re-inscribed by the repeated invocation of authorized knowers, including criminologists and politicians, and legitimated by interviews with a former Vancouver detective who openly acknowledged that scant resources were dedicated to the disappearances and that tips, including one linking some of the missing women to the Pickton farm, were often not pursued vigorously or were ignored altogether (Matas 2002a).

By February 23, 2002, however, two first-degree murder charges had been issued and the focus of coverage shifted decisively away from the offences of the police and toward those of the accused himself. From February 23 to 27, 2002, the negligence narrative was consigned to the margins of the coverage and considered directly only once in a *Globe and Mail* editorial. During this period, information about the police largely chronicled the daunting task of accumulating evidence in a challenging and unconventional crime scene. Accordingly, the established image of a selectively responsible and selectively protective police force was eroded by a sustained focus on the hyper-professionalism and scientific precision of those carrying out the forensic investigation. Thus, from the arrest forward, the negligence narrative began to lose its central positioning and, while it never fully vanished from the coverage, it did not return with the same vigour that characterized its initial articulation.

Yet in spite of its fading centrality, the significance of this narrative should not be underestimated — particularly given its preliminary potency. Hall et al. (1978: 58–59) argue that early definitions frequently provide the "primary interpretation" of a news story, offering explanations which "command the field ... in subsequent treatment" and install an interpretive framework which is "extremely difficult to alter fundamentally" once it has been established. If we accept this logic, then we must consider the negligence narrative as more than a short-lived set of stories, a blip on the media radar. On the contrary, we might consider it as one of the key paradigms through which the crisis of the missing women was rendered intelligible to national audiences; it is a formative and tone-setting discourse. Through its clear delineation of a culpable party, the negligence narrative began to offer a coherent way of understanding there was no comprehensive state response as the list of missing women continued to swell for more than two decades. In other words, it operated to define negligent policing as a key problem and thus provided a framework through which the tragedy might become understandable. Its early centrality in the coverage shaped the contours of the debate; it helped to define the limits of how the crisis might be understood and who might be considered complicit in it.

A close analysis of the coverage offers compelling evidence to support this thesis. It is in the sixteen news stories, columns and editorials that consider the effects of police negligence that we find the vast majority of claims implicating the state in the violence of the crisis. The most critical recurring voices — family members Rick Frey and Maggie DeVries, and the prominent criminologist John Lowman — are largely confined to these articles. Frey's interventions — when not limited to narrations of grief — are primarily condemnations of selective policing. In one statement he laments what he perceives to be an official spirit of dismissal: "I'm sure the thought was 'it's another druggie, who cares'" (Girard 2002e). In another, he remarks "we felt ignored and brushed aside and we felt Marnie was being brushed aside because people just saw her as a drug addict and a prostitute" (*Toronto Star* 2007d). DeVries challenges this same culture of negligence. In one paradigmatic quotation, she asked of police performance: "if they're behaving like that with this case, then how is it with everything else? Everyone in Vancouver should be concerned about this" (Armstrong 2002b). Elsewhere she contends that if women from another part of Vancouver had gone missing with the same frequency, "there would be mayhem ... there would be searches and media interest and rewards" (*Globe and Mail* 2002). Lowman echoes these sentiments. In one article, he argues: "clearly those responsible for the investigation did not show as much concern about the health and safety of the prostitutes than they should have" (Girard 2002e). And elsewhere: "the information out there gives the impression [the police] did not make this a priority the way it should have been" (Hume and Bailey 2002). What is particularly notable about these quotations, and the negligence narrative more generally, is that they tend to appear in relative isolation. That is, they articulate one very specific way that the state was complicit in the tragedy — police failure — but they do so in a way that occludes the roles of other forms of state violence in reproducing marginality, namely the conditions produced by the law, receding systems of social solidarity and the ongoing effects of racism and colonialism (all of which I discuss in the following chapter).[2] As the only sustained criticism of the state in the coverage, these narratives operate to minimize other factors through a univocal stressing of this single causal condition.

In considering the implications of this one-dimensionality, it is worth returning to the suggestion that primary interpretations often produce a framework which comes to "command the field" of other narrations by setting an ideological limit. I want to suggest that the negligence narrative constitutes such a framework and operates to limit the possibility of a broader analysis. By producing the sex worker as a subject fundamentally alienated from the protection of the police, these narratives lend themselves to a coherent, if facile, way of explaining how so many women could be taken without eliciting an aggressive response by the state. To the degree that the state can be held accountable, negligence is defined as *the* problem and the crisis takes on a degree of analytic closure. Importantly, the demands for redress and political change scattered throughout the coverage are primarily focused on police protection, demanding that people on the margins of society be equal recipients of its assurances. Moreover, calls for a public inquiry into the way the investigation was handled tend to promote such a process as a way of understanding and ultimately rectifying the culture of dismissal that defined the police reaction. With the field of analysis so defined, solutions are largely restricted to strategies that would make law enforcement institutions more accountable by ensuring that they specifically include the marginalized and the street-involved under the umbrella of their protection. Demands are primarily articulated as demands for recognition of the unrecognized. The spirit of these claims is powerfully evidenced by a post-conviction editorial that appeared in the *Toronto Star*. Here, the editors surmised that if "any good comes of the Pickton case, it is that mainstream society and its institutions will hopefully pay attention more quickly when people on the fringes come to harm" (*Toronto Star* 2007a). Focused as it is on winning attention for those on the "fringes," such an analysis fails to interrogate the existence of the fringe itself.

The critique limits itself to improving the experience of being marginalized and brackets the larger imperative of erasing marginality altogether. We see here one of the core dangers of over-emphasizing the negligence paradigm. Such a move privileges questions of recognition even as it occludes questions of redistribution (Fraser 1995).

The point here is not to deny the significance of police mismanagement. On the contrary, it is important to recognize the key role that this official disregard played in reproducing the conditions of endangerment in which the victims worked. Rather, I wish to underscore the limits of an analysis that explains this heinous set of crimes as a simple coupling of irresponsible policing with the psychopathic practices of a serial killer. While there is some acknowledgement of violence as an everyday reality for street-level sex workers (discussed at length in Chapter Four), taken in its totality the coverage tends to reproduce this superficial binary.

I want to stress that the negligence narrative itself is not reducible to one simple uninterrupted form. Within this narrative, there are divergent explanations of neglect. Some accounts privilege individual abdications of responsibility, signaling the personal failure of the "few unscrupulous men" who refused to take a growing crisis seriously, an approach which isolates individual actors as culpable (Razack 2004).[3] Other accounts privilege structural explanations, pointing to a lack of information-sharing between police forces and other bureaucratic impediments as the barriers that stalled an adequate response (see Matas 2002a, for example). What both kinds of explanations have in common is that they produce a problem that is *manageable*. Whether the problem is the few bad apples that shirked their responsibilities or the series of inefficient or error-laden bureaucratic practices that endangered a certain population, relatively simple political reconfigurations might be employed as solutions. Answers exist within the established political order. Through this logic, an irresponsible mayor can be (and was) voted out of office, police leadership can be replaced and policing practices can be refined and made more accountable. But as long as this critique remains contained within the spheres of individual responsibility and bureaucratic bungling, it poses little threat to the legitimacy of the prevailing political order.

The advent of the Pickton trial and the intense media interest that enveloped it created the potential for a thorough public consideration of the full dimensions of the crisis of the missing and murdered women. Such an analysis might have presented a compelling challenge to liberal-pluralist assumptions about the universality of state protection. Yet despite the marked presence of narratives that identified specific forms of state negligence, the coverage operated to effectively manage the state's culpability in the tragedy by privileging police negligence as definitive, while omitting other forms of state complicity in their narrations.

Notes

1. Section 7 of the *Canadian Charter of Rights and Freedoms* (1982) establishes that every citizen has the right to "life, liberty and security of the person and the right not to be deprived thereof except in accordance with the principles of fundamental justice."

2. Notably, however, both Maggie DeVries and John Lowman have been outspoken critics of these larger factors elsewhere. In *Missing Sarah*, a published memoir of her sister's life, in testimony before a House of Commons subcommittee, and elsewhere, DeVries has been critical of the state's role in endangering street-level sex workers. She has been a strident advocate of public policy changes that would allow street-involved women to gain control over their own bodies and the conditions of their own work. Lowman, moreover, has been one of the most prominent advocates of prostitution law reform, arguing throughout a sprawling body of work that the state has been complicit in violence against sex workers in a number of important ways. Yet these more profound structural criticisms are all but absent from the coverage. Where they do appear, it is primarily through veiled or implied statements, with direct criticisms confined to a few marginal spaces within the coverage; criticisms of the state are almost exclusively articulated as criticisms of police negligence.

3. In the introduction to *Dark Threats White Knights*, Razack interrogates the "official story" of Canadian violence in Somalia, which installs the image of a "gentle, peacekeeping nation betrayed by a few unscrupulous men" as explanatory. Her interest in the ways that 'bad apple' narratives (which produce individual transgressors as aberrations in otherwise accountable institutions) work to camouflage the operation of hegemonic systems of subordination strikes an important note of harmony with this project.

Chapter 2

Absolving the State

The law, in its majestic equality, forbids the rich as well as the poor to sleep under bridges, to beg in the streets, and to steal bread. — Anatole France, 1894

The coverage's core explanations of the crisis of missing and murdered women limit the ways in which the state might be considered complicit in the tragedy. As we have seen, narrations of state culpability are primarily limited to themes of negligence which privilege disinterested or unaccountable authorities as a key explanation. I want now to dispute the sufficiency of such narrations by examining three central ways that the state has operated to imperil marginalized women in British Columbia. I argue below that sweeping retrenchments of state systems of social solidarity after 1983, amendments to the Criminal Code targeted at curbing street prostitution and the persistent effects of state colonial policy are foundational to the distinct set of dangerous conditions in which most of the missing and murdered women lived and worked.

The analysis that follows has two objectives. The first is to establish specific ways that state practices have operated to imperil street-involved women. The second is to examine the degree to which those policies are examined in print narratives that have sought to explain the crisis to their readership. More precisely, I look at two forms of dispossession. The first is the direct dispossession of personal security that is created by state policies that marginalize and endanger. The second is the indirect dispossession that is made manifest through the creation of an "ideological absence which is then made material" (Burk 2006: 50). In other words, explanations of the crisis that omit or minimize state complicity have the ideological effect of dispossessing the victims of the experience of that violence. The erasure of specific state culpabilities naturalizes their violence, an ideological process that works to legitimate their material perpetuation. As key agents in the construction of our knowledge about events and institutions that are central to establishing the "boundaries of public discourse," news narratives are particularly well placed to shape how the crisis is understood by broad audiences. As such, they are particularly well placed to "explain, rationalize and resolve [the] unsupportable contradictions and tensions" that are at the core of the state's role in the crisis (Henry and Tator 2002: 235). In the analysis that follows, I attempt to unmask three of these contradictions and the ideological commitments that camouflage them. Before doing so, however, I want to be clear that the ordering of these arguments should not be taken as an indication of their importance. It should go without saying, for example, that state violence against Aboriginal people is not simply a function of neoliberal capitalism. It is important to point out that the very foundations of the Canadian state are rooted in a process of dispossession and each of the contradictions that I discuss below corresponds in one way or another to those violent beginnings.

The Violent Rise of the Neoliberal State

The social and material dangers of poverty in British Columbia — and especially the acute variants found in the Downtown Eastside — are inseparable from the sweeping political developments that have occurred in the province over the last three decades. The emergence of a new politics of the right and the retrenchment of established systems of social assurance correspond closely with the period in which so many women were taken from the Downtown Eastside. While the relationship between these phenomena is not exclusively causal, explanations of the crisis of the missing and murdered women that occlude these political considerations risk camouflaging key ways that state practices were complicit in the tragedy.

State social programs designed to ensure a basic level of equality and security — what I refer to as the "state structures of social solidarity" throughout this book — have been very publicly under siege in British Columbia since Premier Gordon Campbell was elected to the provincial legislature with a commanding majority mandate in 2001. Yet the rise of a new right politics — of which Campbell's Liberals are only the most recent and radical standard bearers — has its origins in a process of disintegration that began in earnest decades earlier. The gradual disillusionment of the "post-war settlement" — a de-facto pact of non-aggression between capital, labour and the state born of the economic turmoil of the 1930s and wrought in the political tumult of the 1940s — is intractably connected to changes in global markets that occurred in the 1970s. In Canada, as elsewhere, the "settlement" had produced a vast architecture of state structures of social assurance. Many of the policies that have become synonymous with the Canadian welfare state were crafted in the post-war period; single-payer universal healthcare, national pensions, old-age security schemes and a host of other policies designed to redistribute wealth and provide a certain level of universal assurance were all products of this era. These were social gains that many thought irreversible as the model of the large interventionist state proved remarkably proficient in the 1950s and 1960s (Palmer 1986).

Yet by the end of the 1960s, the high rates of growth that had defined the economies of advanced capitalist countries had begun to be threatened by surging levels of unemployment and inflation (Harvey 2005). Canada's competitiveness in global markets began to decline sharply as inflation eroded the desirability of Canadian products and unit labour costs continued to rise above those of its major trading partners. British Columbia's resource-reliant economy suffered more than others, as industrialized countries began to rely increasingly on cheaper materials from elsewhere. As inflation and the national debt spiraled out of control in the mid 1970s, Pierre Trudeau's Liberal federal government sought relief through reductions in real wages and a new emphasis on restraint (Palmer 1986). Crisis had afforded the opportunity for a dramatic new political realignment; as Bryan Palmer (1986: 14) has observed, it was precisely the "mushrooming character of the budgetary deficits" that "provided the ideological and economic legitimation for the rise of the political right." Considered in this way, we are reminded that the process of social disintegration that has its roots in the crises of the 1970s was not inevitable but the product of a series of calculated political decisions. As Hall (1983: 23) observes of the rise of Thatcherism in the United Kingdom — a realignment born of similar conditions — "political and ideological work is required to disarticulate old formations... the 'swing to the right' is not a reflection of the crisis: it is itself a *response* to the crisis" [emphasis in original].

Realignments inaugurated in the 1970s and early 1980s paved the way for the ascendancy of a pervasive new politics of neoliberalism, albeit with varying levels of enthusiasm in different jurisdictions. With the deregulation and opening of global markets and the welfarist models increasingly disparaged as obsolete, states began to adopt new strategies to best position their economies and societies to compete in the international marketplace. The raft of devotees to this philosophy that were elected in the early 1980 — notably in the United States, the United Kingdom and Canada — championed the "competition state" and sought to replace regulation with flexibility, protective tariff schemes with free trade and state structures with private enterprise. Marked by a defined hostility toward the interventionism of the "big state," these regimes of the new right imagined a world where the market was central and governments were relatively distant, acting merely as the providers of a basic social and political infrastructure while ensuring the reproduction of a stable environment for accumulation. As Stephen McBride and Kathleen McNutt (2007) observe of neoliberalism, the state is decreasingly able to act as a "decommodifying hierarchy" with the capacity to take certain activities out of the market; by contrast, it acts increasingly as a "collective commodifying agent" by transferring a growing number of its functions to private enterprise. In other words, the state has become less and less interested in classifying certain practices and programs as too important to be subjected to the uncertainty of market forces. Strategies of redistribution and programs of universal assurance have increasingly given way to modes of governance that emphasize personal responsibility and flexibility through a "valorization of the rational economic actor and market relations" (Brodie 1999: 43). Neoliberal philosophies of public management have worked to redefine well-being as an individual or family responsibility rather than a collective "communitarian" enterprise. Individuals — like the market — are expected to be self-reliant and relatively autonomous from the state. As Nancy Fraser (2003: 163) puts it, the neoliberal citizen is understood as an "actively responsible agent" who, as a "subject of (market) choice and a consumer of services" is invested with the obligation to "enhance her quality of life through her own decisions;" she is rendered an "expert on herself, responsible for managing her own human capital to maximal effect." The two-fold result of this shift is an increased reliance on individual solutions to public problems and the emergence of state approaches to social policy that privilege fiscal considerations above all others (Morrow et al. 2004).

Since the early 1980s a procession of provincial governments in British Columbia have demonstrated — with varying degrees of zeal — an allegiance to the politics of neoliberalism. Their predecessors in the post-war period, a mix of conservative and social democratic regimes, had presided over an expansionist process of "province building," marked by the creation of a large provincial civil service, a sweeping project of accumulation grounded in mass production and mass consumption, major investments in social infrastructure and, by 1975, a relatively progressive labour code (Palmer 1986). But the crisis born of the recession of 1981–1982 acted as a key pretext for the "phased abandonment" of this model as the right-aligned Social Credit government of Bill Bennett was re-elected on a controversial platform of "restraint" in 1983 (Carroll and Ratner 1989). In the ensuing years, the British Columbian state embarked on a dramatic process of unraveling the social gains of the post-war period. The notorious 1983 budget introduced a bundle of new legislation designed to take aim at the rights of organized labour and begin the process of hollowing out the state's social infrastructure.[1] The budget lit a fuse and an unprecedented mass-mobilization organized to confront it. In the months of confrontation that followed — most notably in the fall of 1983, when an opposition calling itself Operation Solidarity mobilized hundreds of thousands in an "epic battle" against the regime that would last 130 days — the state demonstrated its willingness to use coercion in the defense of its "crisis-management" strategy (Palmer 1986). By 1987, however, a series of compromises and public relations failures effectively muted the popular opposition. The repressive state activism of 1983 began to give way to a "more expansive hegemonic project" constructed around a "right populist appeal" to consumerist notions of "public interest" and libertarian notions of democracy (Carroll and Ratner 1989).

Social Credit's revolution in the 1980s had so altered the terms of governance that by the time the centre-left New Democratic Party (NDP) was elected to govern in 1991, a new set of structural limitations had been constructed, tightly constraining social democratic ambitions within its boundaries. The party did accomplish some modest gains but its leadership found itself rigidly constricted on questions of capital accumulation in an increasingly globalized marketplace. As they governed through to 2001, pressures to pursue a policy of "fiscal discipline" pushed them to reproduce many of the strategies championed by their predecessors. By 1993, for example, the NDP government had abandoned its traditional solidarity with marginalized peoples and reinvigorated the campaign against social assistance recipients, unleashing a less dramatic but still robust set of welfare cuts by 1995. For Carroll and Ratner (2005: 189), the political changes wrought by the NDP showed that the "stricture of not alienating the business community" had become a central concern.

What might have seemed a "discernable if reluctant" engagement with neoliberalism under the NDP gave way to an enthusiastic embrace of the ideology and a return to right militancy with the election of Gordon Campbell's Liberals in 2001 (McBride and McNutt 2007: 177). As Social Credit had in the 1980s, the Liberals embarked on a decidedly radical program of reformation, a process that would include the single deepest cuts to social spending in Canadian history (Carroll and Ratner 2005). Following the introduction of a sweeping set of tax reductions — an initiative that created the largest deficit in the province's history — the Liberals sought to streamline the state by gutting some its core social functions. Few programs were immune to cutting but income assistance was among the most aggressively targeted. Welfare spending was slashed by 30 percent — $581 million over three years — while an unprecedented new set of restrictions were imposed on recipients, including changes to who was to be considered "employable" and time limits on eligibility. The Canadian Centre for Policy Alternatives called it "a bad time to be poor" as some recipients had their already meager incomes reduced by as much as $395 per month (Klein and Smith 2006). McBride and McNutt (2007) observe that a series of "disquieting trends" followed these reductions, as thousands lost their eligibility. For example, food bank usage and homelessness surged. Meanwhile, a series of childcare programs were terminated, childcare subsidies were reduced and the three government ministries responsible for children — including the Ministry of Community, Aboriginal and Women's Services — suffered a cumulative budget reduction of $843 million from 2001–2004. At the same time, employment equity programs were cancelled, medical premiums went up, access to legal aid services was reduced and the universal prescription drug program was converted into an income-based pharmacare plan. These sweeping retrenchments of the social safety net were premised on the state's oft-trumpeted objective of creating a culture of "self-sufficiency." In rhetoric and deed they promoted new forms of "active citizenship" constructed in contrast to "dependency" on the state. This ideological commitment drove efforts to redefine personal well-being as an individual and not a social concern and acted as the key justification of the state's attempts to withdraw from the business of providing basic social guarantees (Klein and Smith 2006). Within the ambit of Canadian federalism, however, sub-national governments like British Columbia's are not the sole arbiters of state policy; provincial decision-making is always disciplined by developments at the federal level and increasingly by global structures and markets. The rise of this particular variant of neoliberalism is thus irrevocably connected to broader national shifts. It is rooted in a series of decisive renegotiations of the federal-provincial relationship inaugurated in the mid 1990s. The federal Liberals came to power in 1993 calling for a militant crusade against the massive budgetary deficits that had plagued their predecessors. Once elected, they demanded temporary austerity while they returned the country to fiscal order. With their 1995 budget, they slashed funding for health, education and social welfare by 25 percent, leaving provincial and municipal governments with the necessity of dramatically altering service delivery.[2] Jean Chretien's Liberal government did manage to eliminate the inherited deficit but there has been little restoration of social spending as servicing the national debt and "tax relief" have become the favored targets of the large budgetary surpluses that were consistently recorded until Canada sunk back into deficit in 2009 (Russell and Dufour 2007). Janine Brodie (1999: 42) has observed that former federal governments can "claim a victory against the deficit largely because [they] shifted monies from insurance schemes… and shifted the financial burden of social policy to the provinces."

What was rationalized as short-term austerity in 1995 soon became the status-quo as the federal government adjusted to embrace the new ideological "consensus" that championed market liberalization and a shrinking state as the cornerstones of economic prosperity. In the process of this reconfiguration the Canadian state has hastened the neoliberalization of sub-national governments. For McBride and McNutt (2007), the millennial radicalism of British Columbia's ruling Liberals is but a mimicking of a process that occurred federally in the 1990s. In their view, the province lies at the end of a chain of national and supra-national influences. Public consent for Gordon Campbell's reformist zeal is necessarily linked to the "ideological and policy environment apparent at the global and continental level… which facilitated Canada's adjustment to neoliberalism" in ways which allowed or encouraged sub-national governments to follow suit (McBride and McNutt 2007: 194).

The effects of neoliberal restructuring have been acutely felt by British Columbia's most impoverished, many of whom live and work in the Downtown Eastside. Economic marginalization has grown in British Columbia since 1983 and low-income people have become more susceptible to the series of physical and social dangers associated with limited economic power. By 2006, more than 13 percent of British Columbians were living on low incomes, a figure nearly three percentage points higher than national averages and poverty rates in the province have remained significantly higher than in any other province (Klein et al. 2008). Street-level sex workers who operate in the Downtown Eastside — a constituency of which nearly all of the missing and murdered women were a part — are not merely affected by these trends, but their ranks have also been swollen by them. Research conducted by the Pivot Legal Society in 2004 concludes that many who work in the neighbourhood's street-level sex industry do so to compensate for inadequate social assistance. Even those who are able to get beyond the stringent vetting process required to establish welfare eligibility face assistance rates which have slipped significantly below Statistics Canada's low-income cut-off rates, beneath which "people are forced to spend almost all their income on food, shelter

[and] clothing" (Pivot Legal Society 2004). These problems are particularly acute for those receiving social assistance; recent research demonstrates that welfare income for a lone-parent family is more than 50 percent below the official poverty line (*BC Campaign 2000* 2009). Accordingly, many are forced to look elsewhere for additional sources of income. The possibilities of finding licit work are severely truncated by structural barriers (including basic difficulties like consistent access to a phone, childcare, work clothes and money to pay for public transportation) (Pivot Legal Society 2004: 13–14). The challenges of securing employment are significant for those with scant resources and many have turned to prostitution as a means of providing basic necessities for themselves and their families. Contrary to widely held views that insist that those working in prostitution do so to support a drug addiction, Culhane (2003: 596) observes that such assertions often invert perceptions of the situation. She notes:

> poverty is identified as the *outcome* of drug addiction… poverty is rarely analyzed as a causal condition that gives illicit drug use and sex work their particular public character and devastating consequences in this place, at this time.

Indeed, poverty itself creates precarious conditions for those who shoulder its burdens. Income level is well established as a primary determinant of psychological and physical well-being and those without means experience worse health than other Canadians. Parents living in poverty are more likely to lose custody of their children (Pivot Legal Society 2004). Those without means or access to systems of support are also far less likely to find adequate housing. Not surprising is the fact homelessness in Vancouver has increased by an estimated 131 percent since 2002 (Greater Vancouver Richmond District 2008).

A wide diversity of research demonstrates that impoverished people have become increasingly vulnerable in the province since neoliberal policies began to aggressively reshape state structures in 1983. It is crucial to recognize the political dimension of these shifts; if we acknowledge that poverty exposes people to precarious conditions then we must acknowledge that state policies that leave poverty unchecked or increase its prevalence operate to endanger low-income people. If marginalization was the common denominator shared by the missing and murdered women and the restructurings have served to marginalize, then there is reason to expect that the conditions of endangerment that presupposed the crisis continue to persist and have likely been amplified.

There is, however, some consideration of poverty in the coverage. With relative frequency, all three sources describe the missing and murdered as impoverished people who lived in an impoverished neighbourhood. Yet more significant than the mere presence of such descriptions is the particular context of their utterance. The relentless branding of sex workers as members of a deviant, addicted caste — a phenomenon that I consider in detail in the following chapter — overshadows broader considerations of the state's role in reproducing marginality and economic insecurity. Even the most sympathetic accounts — the best of which challenge the stigmatization of sex workers and consider the role of public policy in the crisis directly — tend to re-centre the provocative coupling of "drug addict and prostitute" in their analyses. In one such account, the *Toronto Star*'s lead reporter argues that the characterization of sex workers as "dirty [and] debauched" is instrumental to their classification as a disposable population by authorities and the broader public (DiManno 2007b). Yet as she bemoans this branding, the author herself re-centres deviant practices as the core explanation for the women's vulnerability even as she enumerates the multiple "societal ills" that are brought to bear upon street-involved women. She writes:

> The protracted mass murder of these women is not singularly about prostitution. There are plenty of societal ills that transected, creating a fetid environment for survival sex where women sell their bodies for a pittance, for drugs. Poverty, homelessness, addiction, abandonment, abuse and neglect. (DiManno 2007b)

Thus even in this enumeration, which appears amidst a rare journalistic effort to restore dignity to this "invisible" legion of the "cavalierly dismissed," drug dependency is installed as the central cause of their imperilment and the primary motivation for "survival sex." Indeed, themes of narcotic dependency stand as a powerful backdrop throughout the coverage, even tempering the few articles that attempt a broader analysis of how sex workers are rendered vulnerable. Of the 156 articles that I examined, only two attempted substantive considerations of the role of state social policy in endangering street-level workers. The most thorough of these appeared in the *Globe and Mail* under the secondary headline, "Root causes remain the same." Author Mark Hume (2007) insists that the crisis of the missing and murdered women is about more than the atrocities committed by a serial killer. He invokes neighbourhood activist Harsha Walia at length, allowing her quotations to link dramatic reductions in state social spending to spiraling levels of poverty, homelessness, child apprehension and a generalized vulnerability in the neighbourhood. Yet the article's critical tone is tempered by its final paragraphs. Beneath a jarring photograph of a women staring out vacantly from her spot on a Downtown Eastside sidewalk, the article concludes:

> A few hours after the Pickton verdict came down yesterday, a young woman who wouldn't give her name, squatted on a sidewalk on East Hastings, near the intersection with Gore Avenue ... The woman looked glassy-eyed and when she was asked what she thought of the verdict, she nodded her head loosely and answered: "crack?" For $20 she would have gotten in a car and driven away with anyone. (Hume 2007)

The provocative conclusion of Hume's article underscores the centrality of individual transgression in the explanations of the crisis that suffuse the coverage. Vulnerability is repeatedly conceived as the inevitable outcome of dangerous lifestyle decisions, as the unfortunate but unavoidable corollary of the decision to become involved in the inner city's illicit underworld. Economic marginalization, in this schema, is produced as the effect and not the cause of participation in prostitution and illicit drug markets.

There are considerable consistencies between this privileging of individual "lifestyle choices" and the ideological foundations of the politics of neoliberalism. Both hold the individual actor as fundamentally responsible for their own well-being while playing down — or disregarding altogether — the role of the state and its public policies in countering individual destitution. When poverty is individualized it is divested of connections to the larger political economy to which it corresponds. So understood, solutions to vulnerability become conceived as individual and not public solutions.

Yet, beyond this privileging of individual responsibility, it is the cynical characterization of poverty and destitution as inevitable that demonstrate the most pronounced congruence between the coverage and a neoliberal world view. The repeated characterization of the Downtown Eastside as a drain on the public purse — described as a "poverty sinkhole" where predatory individuals develop "poverty empires" — coupled with the repeated assertion that the core problems have persisted "despite the best intentions of police and politicians over the years" implies that public attempts to eliminate economic marginalization are likely doomed to failure with a population more interested in scoring drugs than taking control of their own lives (DiManno 2007a). In fairness, there are a large number of social service agencies concentrated in the Downtown Eastside, some of which rely on public funding (Smith 2003). The vast majority, however, are underfunded providers of emergency services — food banks, soup kitchens and counseling centres, for example — that act as vital stopgaps against devastation but do little to counter the foundations of vulnerability. Through its fixation on violent exchanges between predatory individuals and drug-addicted prostitutes, a theme to which I return in detail below, the coverage masks the predatory violence of the state itself, whose adherence to the individualized politics of neoliberalism continues to erode the possibility of erecting structures which ensure basic standards of well-being.

Criminal Law and the Attack on Street Prostitution

The coverage also operates to obscure state culpability in the tragedy by minimizing the effects of the criminal law on the working conditions of street-level sex workers. While prostitution *per se* is not illegal in Canada, a series of Criminal Code provisions target it indirectly, rendering it effectively impossible to sell sex without transgressing the law. Sections 210–13 criminalize communication for the purposes of selling sex, living off the "avails" of a sex worker, the keeping of a "common bawdy house," transporting individuals for the purposes of purchasing or selling sex and procuring the services of a sex worker.

It is important to put the current law in some historical context. While prostitution itself has never been a crime in Canada, it has always been regulated indirectly. The current legal controls were raised from the ashes of the old vagrancy laws, repealed in 1972. Under the decidedly gendered previous regime, any woman who could not account for her presence in public spaces ran the risk of being prosecuted as a "common prostitute." The vagrancy provisions were widely interpretable and gave law enforcement almost infinite latitude to determine who might be considered in violation of the law. Yet as Deborah Brock (1998: 6) has observed, cultural shifts that began to emerge in the post-war period initiated a process of sweeping political and social change and "the Canadian state was forced to take an increasingly active role to maintain its hegemony in the face of movements for social and sexual liberation." Accordingly, the state initiated a major overhaul of the Criminal Code in the 1970s; new prostitution legislation was designed to curb the perceived public "nuisance" of prostitution, abandoning its previous focus on moral transgression. To this end, new legislation set its sights on the act of "solicitation" itself. While the act of prostitution remained technically legal, the necessary step of negotiating a transaction was now forbidden by law. But soon courts began to struggle with the interpretation of what constituted "solicitation" and judges across the country had to decide whether a suggestive gesture could constitute a criminal violation (Brock 1998). The Supreme Court offered some clarification in 1978. In *R vs. Hutt* they ruled that "solicitation" must be both "pressing and persistent" and that a single gesture or proposition was no longer sufficient to merit prosecution. While the decision did not strike the law down, it did make it harder to enforce (Fraser 1985; Brock 1998).

The view that prostitution was becoming a widespread crisis gained momentum in the years that followed as arrests under the "solicitation" provision dwindled and municipal attempts to control street prostitution were deemed *ultra vires* (outside of their jurisdiction) in several court decisions. The media played an important role in the construction of this social problem. The *Toronto Star*, for example, ran a series of articles in 1984 entitled, "The Prostitution Crisis," where they claimed that commercial sex was fast becoming an un-policed fixture of the urban landscape (Brock 1998). Yet as both Lowman and Brock have argued, the *Hutt* decision alone is insufficient to explain the spread of street prostitution after 1978. They observe that deepening economic recession, a contracting female labour pool and police crackdowns on the indoor trade (which, in Vancouver, pre-date the *R. Vs. Hutt* decision) were all complicit in driving sex workers to the streets (Lowman 2000). Nevertheless, the ruling was largely blamed for an increased presence of prostitutes on the streets and interest groups (primarily neighbourhood groups) forced the state to take new action.

In 1983 the federal Ministry of Justice appointed a commission to study the state of prostitution. The Fraser Committee, as the commission came to be known, would ultimately report that Criminal Code sections 210–13 were often "contradictory and self defeating" (Lowman 2004: 147). They called for an overhaul of the state's strategy, recommending that some of its restrictions be relaxed. But their recommendations failed to persuade, and in 1985 the Conservative government of Brian Mulroney pursued a different approach, repealing the "solitication" law and replacing it with a more stringent restriction on "communication" for the purpose of selling sex while expanding criminality to both sex worker and client.

The changes to the law introduced in 1985 have created a distinct set of dangers for sex workers, particularly at the street level. A wide diversity of research has demonstrated that the new regime (and particularly the "communication" provision in section 213) has hindered workers' abilities to take precautions on the stroll.[3] Researchers, advocates and sex workers appearing before a parliamentary committee charged with reviewing the laws from 2004 to 2006, testified that the restrictions create a situation where workers are forced to operate in isolated conditions at the margins of the urban space in order to avoid the attention of police and residents likely to register complaints.[4] Soliciting clients in such locations is a deliberate strategy to reduce the risk of arrest but it also amplifies the likelihood of robbery, harassment and predation (House of Commons Subcommittee on Solicitation Laws [hereafter SSLR] 2006). Committee witnesses argued that this scattering of workers and the frequent necessity of changing locations has meant that sex workers have less opportunity to share information with each other, including reports of dangerous clients. They also reported that isolation and fear of arrest forces sex workers to make quick assessments of potential clients and that price and services are much harder to negotiate after getting into a client's car. As Katrina Pacey of the Downtown Eastside's Pivot Legal Society put it:

> Sex workers describe their fear of being caught by police while negotiating the terms of a transaction with a potential client. As a result, they feel rushed in these negotiations and are not able to take the time required to adequately assess a client and to follow their own instincts, or to maybe note if that client is on a bad date list. (SSLR 2006: 65)

Yet Lowman (2000) argues that the laws have also had a cultural effect, operating to further erode the already diminished status of street-level workers, making them even more vulnerable to predation. He links the criminalization of prostitution and the stigma it reproduces to the high rates of homicide committed against street-level sex workers. In testimony before the committee he argued that the communication law has "played a pivotal role in creating a social and legal milieu that has facilitated these homicides," adding that the law itself tends to make women working in the bottom levels of the trade more vulnerable (SSLR 2006).

The application of the current laws has disproportionately affected sex workers

Table 2.1 Prostitution-related incidents reported by police, British Columbia (2003)

Offence	Reported Incidents (2003)	Charges (male)	Charges (female)
Bawdy house (s.210)	15	1	2
Procuring (s.211, 212)	62	15	4
Communication (s. 213)	1822	149	190
Total	1899	165	196

Source: Canadian Centre for Justice Statistics 2004.

operating at the street level. While the street trade accounts for a relatively small part of the overall industry in Canada — estimates range from 5 to 20 percent — police enforcement efforts have been overwhelmingly directed at this sector (SSLR 2006). Justice statistics demonstrate that since being enacted into law, the "communication" provision has accounted for more than 90 percent of prostitution-related offences reported by police (SSLR 2005b). The most recent official survey of Canadian crime statistics confirms the persistence of this pattern. As table 2.1 demonstrates, section 213 accounted for roughly 96 percent of prostitution offences reported by police forces across British Columbia in 2003.

These figures reveal the profound unevenness of enforcement practices. Focused as it is on the public nature of the offence, section 213 targets street-level sex workers almost exclusively, while the other provisions are more commonly used in policing the indoor trade. The marked disparity in application demonstrates that while law enforcement is a constant menace for workers on the stroll, indoor workers are far less likely to be charged. In terms of punishment, comparative studies have also demonstrated that women are affected far more negatively by the enforcement of section 213, a provision which applies to both the client and the seller of sex. While men and women are charged under section 213 with roughly equivalent frequency, women are far more likely to be convicted, incarcerated and sentenced to the maximum penalty. As table 2.2 demonstrates, women were found guilty of "communication" at a rate of 68 percent while men were convicted at a rate of 29 percent; women were sentenced to incarceration in 38 percent of convictions compared to an incarceration rate of 6 percent for men; by contrast, convicted men were spared incarceration and ordered to pay fines in 38 percent of cases compared to a rate of 15 percent for convicted women (SSLR 2005b).

Undoubtedly, the broad category of street prostitution encompasses a wide diversity of experience but it is also the sector in which many of the most impoverished and vulnerable sex workers operate. As the case of the missing and murdered women demonstrates with particular pronouncement, it is in this sector that intersecting systems of subordination — including racism, patriarchy and

Table 2.2 Conviction and Incarceration Rates for Prostitution Offences (2003/2004) – Canada

Sex of Accused	Conviction Rate	Incarceration Rate	Decisions Resulting in Fine as Maximum Penalty
Male/s.213	29%	6%	38%
Male/s.210-213	31%	—	—
Female/s.213	68%	38%	15%
Female/s.210-213	59%	—	—

Source: SSLR 2005a; Kong and Aucoin 2008.

capitalism — interlock most aggressively with law enforcement. As Lowman put it to a parliamentary subcommittee:

> There are all sorts of issues intersecting here — race, class, gender. We don't talk nearly enough about the class issues that are involved here. It's always the lower-class women in prostitution who receive the brunt of law enforcement efforts. (SSLR 2005b)

Prostitution law has been far from an "equal opportunity subordinator," to borrow a phrase from Lisa Sanchez (2004).

Acknowledgement of the imperiling effects of the contemporary legal regime is indispensable to any thorough consideration of the epidemic levels of violence committed against street-involved women in this country. But discussion of the law is decidedly peripheral in the coverage. Only eight of 157 articles make any reference to these sanctions. Of these, six might be considered "critical" in that they question the merit of criminalization or call for some kind of legal reform. Only three of these identify even one way that the law has endangered prostitutes. And only one names a particular law directly. Yet it is not merely the small number of references that is significant here, it is also their location within the coverage. Only one critical reference appears in a news story while four critical references appear in editorials.

Thus the editorial page marks the single site where this theme was considered with any kind of repetition. This trend seems to follow a certain journalistic logic; news stories are intended to provide concise accounts of new developments while editorials are intended to offer opinion and interpretation. In this sense, it seems only fitting that a critical analysis of the law would be confined to the editorial page. Yet such a narrow view — which obscures that news accounts are themselves interpretations, the end products of a process of sorting and selecting — is insufficient to explain the absence of the law in the coverage. The sheer magnitude of coverage — in some cases accounting for more than ten items in a single newspaper edition — meant that news stories provided far more than accounts of daily developments. And while the editorials themselves are important, in one case providing a thoroughly incisive account of the imperiling effects of the "communication" provision, the effectiveness of their critique must be considered within the context of the larger group of narratives (*Globe and Mail* 2007b). When the infrequency of this critique is weighed against the arresting sensationalism of the narratives of drug addiction, serial murder and police negligence that saturate the other pages — repeatedly enunciated by dramatic photographs and headlines — its relative impotence is brought in to sharp relief.

In spite of the relatively small number of critiques of the law that appear in the coverage, the three newspapers demonstrate a far greater willingness to implicate the state in this regard than they do on questions of economic distribution. While the poignancy of these criticisms is certainly minimized by more provocative narratives, it is important to acknowledge that each of the three newspapers does level at least one robust interrogation of the desirability of criminalizing prostitution. Yet in spite of these rare condemnations (in some cases spiked by a hint of righteous indignation), none of the authors acknowledge the law's most disturbing dimension: the radical unevenness of its intent and application.

Though not entirely homogenous, a prevailing logic unifies the six articles that are critical of the law. In general terms, the authors argue that the law itself has failed in its objective to eradicate street prostitution and has had the undesirable effect of making sex work more dangerous. Several call for reform or abolishment of the provisions and some offer theories about why such changes have not yet been effected. In terms of the latter, the most common hypothesis is that a prevailing cultural prudishness or conservatism stands in the way of the decision to liberalize or even legalize prostitution. The *Toronto Star*'s Rosie DiManno (2007b) argues that there is "still too much residual puritanism and paternalism for prostitution to be accepted as a legitimate service profession." An editorial also published by the *Toronto Star* (2007c) proposes similar barriers to reform; it suggests that "the notion of prostitutes working in a safe area or legal brothel offends us, while we accept the fact they work daily in desperate and deadly situations." The *Globe and Mail* (2007b) is more precise in its assessment of why the laws remain on the books. In an editorial that provides the most robust critique of the regulations, they argue that the ruling Conservative party's position that legalization would bring too great a "social cost" has stalled the drive for law reform. The *National Post*, for its part, criticizes the laws but remains agnostic on questions of why they persist.

While these hypotheses are compelling, each provides a characterization of the "problem" that obscures a more fundamental question. By privileging a lingering moralism as the primary barrier to reform, the critical articles operate to reproduce the notion that the violence of the law is born of a prevailing desire to regulate the moral conduct of individuals. Moral condemnation is undoubtedly one dimension of the contemporary regime — a theme I take up more generally in the chapter that follows — but it is decidedly secondary to the law's central preoccupation of spatial control. The most notable achievement of the communication provision (section 213) has not been to eliminate street prostitution but to remove it from certain spaces while containing it in others. The long history of stroll evictions and sex-worker displacements in Vancouver tells us more about the political expediency of protecting certain spaces from "undesirable" populations than it does about a perceived desire to curb certain moral transgressions. The conviction statistics listed above (table 2.1) demonstrate that, in practice, policing has been primarily interested in curbing the visibility of prostitution. Accordingly, street prostitutes — in Vancouver, the most racialized and economically marginalized sector of the industry — not only bear the brunt of police repression, but they are also pushed out of safer spaces and into the isolation of the urban margins. Under the guise of protecting public spaces from dangerous activities, vulnerable individuals are rendered even more vulnerable. As Razack (2002: 9) has argued, the representation of public space as "a unity that must be protected from conflict," presents us with "a compelling example of how we might consider space as a social product by attending to the social hierarchies" that it reveals. Prostitution laws that target public "communication" enshrine sex workers as illegitimate users of the public space while the comparatively *peaceful* behavior of others enshrines them as the "legitimate users and natural owners of the public space" (Razack 2002: 4). I contend that it is primarily prostitution law's ability to 'protect' certain public spaces that accounts for its persistence. As such, analyses of the political challenge of making sex work less vulnerable and that privilege a lingering moralism as a core explanation for the "impasse," offer a limited understanding of the violence of the state's regulation of prostitution.

Colonialism and Its Discontents

State complicity in the crisis is also minimized through the erasure of connections between state violence and the dramatic overrepresentation of Aboriginal women in the grim roster of missing and murdered women. According to an Amnesty International report (2004), Aboriginal women account for roughly one third of the sixty women whose disappearances from the Downtown Eastside were being investigated by police in 2004. Pratt (2005: 1059) puts that figure even higher, arguing that at least thirty-nine of the missing women were Aboriginal. Moreover, many of those whose remains were uncovered on the notorious Port Coquitlam farm were Aboriginal, including four of the six people that Pickton would eventually be convicted of murdering. Consistently, research has demonstrated that Aboriginal women are decidedly overrepresented in the Downtown Eastside's sex trade, including two studies that suggest they account for more than half of all workers in this district (Farley et al. 2005; Currie 1995). Additionally, a study conducted in 2000 for the province's since-eliminated Ministry of Women's Equality found that

Aboriginal women under the age of twenty-six accounted for roughly 70 percent of people working in the neighbourhood's lowest paying prostitution sectors (Culhane 2003: 595). The full significance of these figures does not become clear until the Downtown Eastside's Aboriginal population is weighed against that of the city as a whole. Less than 2 percent of the population of Vancouver identify as Aboriginal, according to the most recent Canadian census figures.[5] The arresting disparity between the relatively small percentage of the population that identify as Aboriginal and the extraordinarily high percentage of Aboriginal women counted among the missing and murdered demands a thorough interrogation. Yet such an interrogation is conspicuously absent in the coverage. Only thirteen of the 156 articles examined make any acknowledgement of the crisis' striking Aboriginal dimension. Moreover, only seven of those references directly acknowledge the Aboriginal heritage of specific victims. Significantly, none of the articles invoke the abundant body of research that clearly demonstrates the disproportionate "burden of social suffering carried by Aboriginal people in this neighborhood" (Culhane 2003).

Taken together, the small group of references fit into two general categories. References in the first grouping are inferential. They acknowledge Aboriginality indirectly, either by alluding to particular cultural signifiers or by offering clues in biographical portraits of the victims. One article, for example, notes that a group of mourners wore "medicine bags… carrying spiritual items," another reports that a victim's mother found comfort in a "smudge ceremony," and another still cites a particular First Nation as the birthplace of one of the victims (Fong 2007; Mickleburgh 2007). References in the second grouping are less suggestive; they note the Aboriginal heritage of some of the victims more directly. These references tended to appear in either short victim biographies or as isolated components of larger statements about the crisis. One such reference, which appeared in a *Globe and Mail* (2002) editorial, is typical of the others; it reads:

> The women who vanished were for the most part prostitutes and drug addicts. Many were Aboriginal. Some were mentally ill. They were part of a much-abused underclass in a derelict part of town, and the main assumption of the police, even as more women disappeared, was that they had left town.

This and similar claims do acknowledge that "many" of the victims were of Aboriginal descent, but they offer no further consideration of what such a statement might imply or why such overrepresentation might be significant. Indeed, not a single article attempts to place Aboriginal overrepresentation in a larger historical context. This alarming set of omissions amounts to nothing short of an erasure of the violent effects that historical and contemporary state policy has had on Aboriginal peoples and communities in British Columbia. Of course, significant media research reminds us that the mainstream press is not in the business of providing historical context. Newspapers are "event-driven" media that tend to focus on the immediate details of a given conflict. The limits of time and space demand that stories be lean and precise. Yet for the purposes of the present study, such arguments are decidedly limited. Far from offering a simple matter-of-fact account of event-based developments, the coverage examined is saturated with background articles, speculative columns and other submissions that go far beyond the conventional limitations of just-the-facts reportage. Narratives about the missing and murdered women which purge the story of its Aboriginal dimension work to simplify and depoliticize the complexities of the case by limiting culpability to a violent criminal, a negligent police force and the self-selected dangers of a street-involved "lifestyle." Such narrations operate to extricate the state from an ever-shrinking list of responsible parties by telling a story from which it is excluded.

The arrival of European settlers in British Columbia brought fundamental and irreversible change to the Aboriginal communities that had occupied those territories for countless generations. Yet, as Jean Barman (1991) insists, it is important to dispense with a vision of pre-contact Aboriginal life that imagines original inhabitants as existing in some sort of static and idyllic state; on the contrary, adaptation to new circumstances was already deeply woven into Aboriginal histories. What altered fundamentally with European contact, however, was the velocity of those developments. In considering the historical relationship between settlers and Indigenous peoples in British Columbia, we must acknowledge a certain degree of cooperation; European trappers, for example, relied heavily on Indigenous knowledge and technology to conduct their trade. Nevertheless, the colonial imposition of a new social and economic order coupled with a prevailing spirit of disregard for Aboriginal peoples did, in turn, produce a devastating set of social and political consequences for the colonized (Barman 1991). The history of European settlement in what is now British Columbia is wrought with dislocations, dispossessions, erasures and a literal decimation of populations. From contact to the present day, Aboriginal peoples have been subjected to pernicious racism that imagined them outside of the dialectic of modern "progress." As Elizabeth Furniss (1995: 15) puts it:

> Native peoples have been perceived not as existing in complex societies, having their own systems of government, their own social and political institutions, and their own highly-developed technologies, but as a child-like, savage race, having only a rudimentary degree of social organization, living a precarious, hand-to-mouth existence, and adhering to superstitious, pagan beliefs.

It was this attitude and the attendant sense of settler entitlement to the land that flowed from it that was at the core of the construction of British Columbia as an inherently white-settler society. As Renisa Mawani (2001: 40) explains, the process of British settlement in the province was not simply about the establishment of a settler colony but rather an attempt to construct a decidedly *white* settler society which was necessarily built on the "attempted genocide and conquest of Aboriginal peoples as well as the importation and exploitation of cheap racialized labor."

The historical record of state participation in specific dislocations and dispossessions of Aboriginal peoples in British Columbia is undeniable. As Barman (2007) demonstrates, multiple levels of government were party — albeit with different levels of participation — in the dubious transactions that drove Aboriginal people out of established communities in Vancouver, particularly in False Creek and the Burrard Inlet peninsula, which is now the site of Stanley Park. Yet, as in other Canadian jurisdictions, these dispossessions extend far beyond the legal and extra-legal expropriation of lands. For example, the Canadian state's unilateral capacity to define who counts as a "status Indian" has held sweeping implications for the determination of who is entitled to inhabit reserve lands, access specific benefits established by the *Indian Act* and a host of other entitlements. Aboriginal women have been particularly vulnerable to the state's power to define "status," as Jo-Anne Fiske (1995) observes. Prior to the 1985 amendments to the *Indian Act*, a woman who married a non-Aboriginal man would both forfeit her own status as well as the status of her children. After the enactment of pernicious legislation in 1951, in fact, a woman losing her status through marriage also lost membership in her local band and her right to reside on reserve lands.

Perhaps the most damaging of the expansive list of state policies that exacted their violence on Aboriginal peoples was the establishment of a network of residential and industrial schools beginning in 1879. The schools, which took Aboriginal children away from their homes on reserve lands and transported them to a network of campuses that were charged with the ominous directive of killing "the Indian" in order to "save the child." The schools were largely administered by church bureaucracies, but, as John Milloy (1999: xii) observes:

> behind every school principal, matron, teacher and staff member who worked in the school system, and behind each participating denomination, stood the Canadian government and the Department of Indian Affairs, which was symbolic of Canada's self-imposed "responsibility" for Aboriginal people set out in section 91: 24 of the British North America Act.

The racist premise on which the schools were established and the traumas born of taking children from their communities are not the only disturbing aspects of the brutal legacy of residential schools. The schools were also defined by patterns of colossal neglect and a widespread tradition of violence and abuse (Milloy 1999). The Leadership Council of the British Columbia Assembly of First Nations observes that the system, which was not entirely abandoned until 1986, has been unparalleled in its impact on Aboriginal communities and peoples. They note that it has produced "breakdown[s] of family cohesion, lack of ability to foster interpersonal relationships, feelings of inferiority, loss of cultural identity and discontinuation of family traditions" in many of the communities that it affected (First Nations Leadership Council of British Columbia 2008). As Milloy (1999: xi) observes:

> it is clear that the schools have been, arguably, the most damaging of the many elements of Canada's colonization of this land's original peoples and, as their consequences still affect the lives of Aboriginal people today, they remain so.

Ward Churchill (2008) takes Milloy's damning assessment even further, arguing that the residential school system and its impacts constitute an act of genocide in accordance with international law. He notes that the 1948 United Nations Convention on the Prevention and Punishment of the Crime of Genocide lists "forcibly transferring children" from one group to another as one of its core definitions of the crime. Significantly, the Canadian parliament omitted this definition when ratifying the convention domestically.

In considering the impacts of these legacies of state violence, it is important to acknowledge the remarkable overrepresentation of Aboriginal peoples in nearly every measured indicator of social and physical suffering in this country. Such figures are particularly striking in Vancouver's Downtown Eastside. Research conducted by regional health authorities at the height of the crisis of missing and murdered women in 1999 gives some indication of the depth of the social, physical and economic challenges that Aboriginal people continue to confront in Vancouver's inner city. In that survey, the Vancouver/Richmond Health Board reported that Aboriginal families are frequently exposed to a "wide prevalence" of risk factors, including inadequate or unsafe housing, widespread unemployment or underemployment, domestic violence and social isolation. They note that 80 percent of Aboriginal children live in poverty and that more than half of Aboriginal families in the region are headed by a lone female parent. Moreover, about half of Vancouver's "children-in-care" (a term that generally refers to children who have been removed from their homes by provincial authorities) are of Aboriginal descent. Infant mortality rates were recorded at levels roughly twice as high as those of the total population while Aboriginal adults were eight times more likely to die from alcohol and narcotics. In fact, their research suggests that this cohort has a life expectancy roughly sixteen years lower than that of its non-Aboriginal counterparts. High levels of HIV infection in Vancouver's inner city, moreover, have had particularly devastating consequences for Aboriginal women who are reported to be more than three times as likely to die from the disease (Vancouver/Richmond Health Board 1999). In spite of efforts to improve the situation — including the reassertion of control over health and social services by Aboriginal people through the establishment of Urban Aboriginal Health Centres — many of these indicators of marginalization have persisted (Benoit et al. 2003). A wide diversity of recent research demonstrates that inadequate housing, exposure to HIV and other communicable diseases, unemployment, addiction, familial abuse, exposure to violence and racism and a significant list of other vulnerabilities continue to affect Aboriginal people more acutely than others in the neighbourhood.

While it would be too simple to posit an exclusively causal relationship between these indicators and the legacies of state violence outlined briefly above, any assessment which omits this dark history defies a growing body of research which notes that the ongoing traumas of colonization continue to have significant affects on Indigenous peoples and communities. In their consideration of the marginalization of Aboriginal sex workers in Vancouver, Farley et al. (2005: 245) argue that "colonization and racism result in extensive and insidious trauma that wears away at its victims' mental and physical health," frequently resulting in symptoms related to post-traumatic stress disorder. Moreover, as the Royal Commission on Aboriginal Peoples (RCAP) identified more than ten years ago, the high incidences of violence recorded in Aboriginal communities are inseparable from the history of colonization in Canada. According to evidence presented at the Commission's hearings, factors contributing to patterns of violence include "the breakdown of healthy family life resulting from residential school upbringing, racism against Aboriginal peoples, [and] the impact of colonialism on traditional values and culture" (Statistics Canada 2006).

These patterns of violence have been decidedly gendered in their effects. Statistics Canada reports that Aboriginal women are significantly more affected — than both Aboriginal men and non-Aboriginal women — by physical and psychological spousal abuse and spousal homicide as well as non-spousal violence, stalking and criminal harassment (Statistics Canada 2006). In fact, domestic violence has been identified as a major cause of Aboriginal migration from reserves and remote communities to urban centres. The RCAP (1984) found that nearly 60 percent of Aboriginal people who migrate to urban areas are female and that family-related reasons (including spousal and familial abuse) were most commonly identified as the motivation for migration. These figures may provide some indication of why, in a neighbourhood where men outnumber women nearly three to one, the Aboriginal population remains roughly balanced along gender lines (Benoit et al. 2003). Significantly, while 6 percent of Vancouver's Aboriginal residents are themselves survivors of residential schools, nearly 65 percent have family members who were "educated" in the system (Statistics Canada 2001). Thus while "it would be shortsighted to see Aboriginal women in the [Downtown Eastside] merely as victims of larger structural forces, without a sense of agency about how to change their situation," as Cecilia Benoit et al. (2003: 824) suggest, it is important to interrogate how legacies of state violence continue to have persistent affects. To acknowledge, that is, that many of the neighbourhood's residents live their lives through a "social cartography" shaped by the "experiences of racism and the reserve system, by the dislocations of residential school and foster care" (Robertson 2007: 529).

Given the striking body of research that identifies Aboriginal people as a particularly marginalized group in the Downtown Eastside, it is difficult to understand why this dimension of the story is so startlingly overlooked in the coverage examined, particularly since so much of this research comes from sources not generally considered controversial by the news establishment, including government reports, studies conducted by Statistics Canada, and other well-established "authorities" not generally considered controversial by the news establishment. For Culhane (2003: 595), the "regime of disappearance" of which this erasure is a symptom is constructed through media practices which privilege the exoticism of drug use and violence over the "mundane brutality of everyday poverty," rely on "scientific" categories that pathologize and medicalize marginalization and demonstrate a pronounced disinterest in the strategies of resistance which emanate from the subjects at the centre of their narratives. At the convergence of these practices, she contends, narrative accounts depoliticize Aboriginal marginalization by stripping it of its historical linkages to colonial state practices and disguising its racial dimension. She writes:

> The thread that ties these themes together in the specific context of Downtown Eastside Vancouver is a particular form of "race blindness." Recognition of the burden of social suffering carried by Aboriginal people in this neighborhood — and in Canada as a whole — elicits profound discomfort in a liberal, democratic nation state like Canada, evidencing as it does the *continuing* effects of settler colonialism, its ideological and material foundations, and its ongoing reproduction. (Culhane 2003: 595)

In building on Culhane's view that a persistent racial blindness informs journalistic practices, I do not argue for a view of media operatives as simple propagandists operating in the interests of a vaguely constituted "dominant group." It is important to reiterate that the view of a prevailing media ideology that informs this study locates domination in the set of "taken-for-granted value commitments and reality judgments [and] assumptions which are naturalized [and] transformed over time" that inform the professional culture of mainstream journalism (Hackett and Carroll 2006: 31). Thus, we might consider the erasure of Aboriginality in the coverage, not as a deliberate strategy of denial but rather as a pattern of signification that is informed by certain "commonsense" assumptions about the nature of Canadian society that erase its sharp racialized divisions — what Henry and Tator (2002) call "democratic racism." That is, it identifies the tendency of "dominant discourses" to operate from a set of assumed norms that imagine Canada as a "White, humanistic, tolerant and accommodating society." Such assumptions erase and naturalize the well- established histories of violence and racism that have underpinned the state's colonial policies, reproducing the view that "because Canadian society [including its formal state structures] upholds the ideals of a liberal democracy, it cannot possibly be racist." Connectedly, the coverage's erasure of Aboriginality — its "race blindness," to put it in Culhane's terms — illustrates how the narratives examined operate to reproduce certain assumptions about the Canadian state. They uphold the view that fundamental ideals of liberal egalitarianism are central to the governance of this country by camouflaging the "insupportable contradictions and tensions" at the core of ongoing colonial state policies (Henry and Tator 2002: 226)

Finally, it is important to acknowledge an inherent danger at the core of analyses like the one I have just provided. By focusing on the effects of state violence on Aboriginal women, there is a risk of re-centring the state and enacting a further erasure of the women themselves. It is crucial to be wary of representations in which "the women fail to appear as active agents or are silenced as victims" (Jiwani and Young 2006: 899). Indeed, the Downtown Eastside is not merely a space where the horrific dramas of repressive policing, abject poverty and neocolonial subordination are played out upon the bodies of a victimized population. By contrast, the neighbourhood remains a fertile ground for resistance and a key site for the elaboration of a politics of decolonization. Overly deterministic analyses, many of which I draw on in this chapter, can have the inadvertent effect of muting resistance by privileging victimization. This is particularly true of the RCAP; as Carmela Murdocca (2009: 30) observes of that process:

> Thinly veiled within the Commission's understanding is that the legacy of colonialism has resulted in a range of "social disorders" endemic to the Aboriginal community. What is produced from this understanding is that "social disorder" is a symptom of colonialism and the task for the criminal justice system is to address the 'symptoms' of cultural degeneracy which inevitably has become the ontological property of Aboriginal peoples in a white settler context.

A full consideration of the three dimensions of state complicity that I outline above demonstrates how news discourses have camouflaged the role of the state in producing the crisis. While it is crucial to heed Gitlin's warning and be wary of overstating the influence of media messages, it is also crucial to interrogate the role that such messages play in shaping imagined understandings of how the state operates in Canada. At their worst, the narratives discussed above reproduce the view that governance in Canada, though imperfect, is essentially guided by prevailing values of tolerance, egalitarianism and benevolence. I contend that the rise of neoliberalism in British Columbia has operated to further marginalize low-income people, the criminalization of prostitution has targeted specific sectors of the industry while allowing others to operate with relative impunity and the state's colonial crimes continue to be of decisive consequence in this country. I argue that all of these political strategies have been complicit in producing a social and political milieu where scores of marginalized women could be made to "disappear" without eliciting a sweeping public outcry (prior to 1999, anyway) and a vigorous response by the state. News discourses that downplay or omit connections between these specific state culpabilities and the crisis itself have the effect of rationalizing and resolving contradictions to the state's claimed commitment to a basic egalitarianism.

Notes

1. For a comprehensive account of the content of the 1983 budget and the related 26 pieces of legislation, see, Palmer, *Solidarity*, 19–24.
2. In addition, the 1995 federal budget reorganized transfer payments to the provinces, scrapping the established Canada Assistance Plan — which earmarked funds for specific social spending categories — replacing it with the Canada Health and Social Transfer which lumped transfers together allowing the provinces to determine specific allocation of funds, a process that, as Brodie and others have observed, effectively eliminated the national state's capacity to ensure universal standards of social security.
3. See for example: House of Commons Subcommittee on Solicitation Laws, *The Challenge of Change: A Study of Canada's Prostitution Laws* (Ottawa: Government of Canada, 2006); Pivot Legal Society, *Voices for Dignity*; Pivot Legal Society, *Beyond Decriminalization: Sex Work, Human Rights, and a New Framework for Law Reform* (Vancouver: Pivot Legal Society, 2006); Lowman, "Violence and the Outlaw Status of (Street) Prostitution."
4. In 2003, the House of Commons adopted a motion to form a subcommittee mandated to review Canada's prostitution laws. From 2004-2006, the Subcommittee on Solicitation Laws (SSLR) conducted hearings across the country. They issued their final report — "The Challenge of Change: A Study of Canada's Criminal Prostitution Laws" — in December 2006.
5. This figure is based on Statistics Canada's 2006 Census of the Canadian population, which recorded a total population of 571,600 in the city of Vancouver Census proper (as opposed to the larger metropolitan area). Within this population, 11,145 people identified as "Aboriginal."

Chapter 3

Producing the Prostitute

The figure of Robert Pickton is unmistakably the central preoccupation of the coverage studied. He is portrayed not only as a cold predator, a raucous binger and a cunning criminal, but also, somewhat contradictorily, as daft and illiterate, a folksy pig farmer noted for his "poor hygiene," pinkish skin and greasy, straggly hair (Fong 2007). These characterizations couple with reports of the offender's grisly history of violence to establish him as an archetypically sinister figure. Yet media interest in Pickton is not restricted to an analysis of the man himself or even the crimes that he committed. Rather, press accounts are decidedly focused on the universe in which he preyed, the spaces in which he trawled and the particular kind of woman that was his victim. Accordingly, the figure of the street-involved sex worker is also indispensable to these accounts. In this chapter, I contend that the coverage provides a coherent framework for understanding who the prostitute is and what, precisely, motivates her (and it is always *her*) sustained participation in the precarious market of the street. It produces her as a "distinguishable social type" (Cohen 2002: 1): a drugged, dazed, deviant, dissolute and corrupted "other" whose affiliation with a notorious underworld places her in constant threat of danger and predation.

Importantly, however, such descriptions are not univocal. More sympathetic portrayals also produce sex workers as victims, not merely of the danger of the stroll, but also of a long history of predatory abuse, personal devastation and all-consuming addiction. They are also produced as members of families, as daughters and wives, as sisters and girlfriends. Yet both in spite of and as a result of these seemingly sympathetic portrayals, the prevailing definitions of the prostitute that emerge from the coverage reproduce and reflect core ideological assumptions about the trade; they elide fundamental considerations about what drives individuals to its lowest sectors. In this, they cohere closely with historical representations that produce sex workers as members of a criminally dangerous and morally corrupt underworld. As I will demonstrate, statements attributed to family and friends of the missing and murdered women, advocates and allies of street-involved women and sex workers themselves contribute to the construction of this larger image. They are central to the establishment of a dominant ideological paradigm, a tightly constricted set of boundaries in which the figure of the prostitute is rendered understandable.

Criminal Danger and Moral Corruption

The iconic figure of the prostitute has historically been assigned a series of divergent popular meanings. As Phillip Hubbard (1999: 1) has observed, sex workers have not only been a source of simultaneous "fear and fascination" in Western societies, they have also been constituted as an affront to established morality and as "nefarious" deviant others. Yet, despite the persistence of this fear, fascination and condemnation, prevailing representations of the essential nature of the prostitute have never been static; they have been transformed by a series of historical permutations. Chris Greer and Yvonne Jewkes (2005: 23) note that "the boundaries separating different categories of deviance and dangerousness are not fixed and immutable, but fluid and permeable; they constantly change as a function of shifting cultural sensibilities and public concern."

A diverse range of identities have been assigned to sex workers by mass-media discourses, characterizations that have resonated to varying degrees in different periods. To note only a few, they have been defined as vectors of disease and contagion, entrapped sexual slaves, morally depraved, criminally culpable, victims of the "white slave trade," endangered persons, "fallen" women, symbols of community failure, "feeble-minded," a public nuisance, an affront to public respectability, unpredictable addicts and deranged individuals (O'Neill et al. 2008; Hallgrimsdotir et al. 2006; Sangster 2001). Of course, many of these labels have long vanished from popular usage and remain relevant only as residues of abandoned discourses. Nevertheless, contemporary media narratives have privileged their own set of characterizations that establish prostitutes as "distinguishable types" — as particular kinds of "folk devils" — which retain much of the fear and loathing expressed by earlier iterations (Cohen 2002: 1). I want to turn now to two such stigmatizations that persist: the prostitute as a source of danger and criminal deviance and the prostitute as a symbol of moral corruption. Both are central aspects of the coverage.

Representations that romanticize and celebrate the figure of the prostitute as a symbol of vivacious hedonism and sexual liberation have long been countered by a persistent association of commercial sex with a sinister underworld of danger and criminality. As Erin Van Brunschot et al. (1999: 48) put it: "the obverse of the 'whore with a heart of gold' is the depraved, dissolute and deviant image of the prostitute." Since at least the nineteenth century, street prostitution or "kerb-crawling" has been associated with distinct forms of urban deviance. Judith Walkowitz (1992: 21), for example, notes in her survey of prostitution in late-Victorian London that the figure of the street prostitute operated as a "public symbol of female vice." For Van Brunschot et al. (1999), elements of this nineteenth century image persist in contemporary depictions. In considering prostitution narratives in Canadian newspapers from 1981–1995, they report a sustained conflation of prostitution with deviance and criminality, accented by an assumed seamlessness between street-level sex work and narcotic dependency. Helga Hallgrimsdottir et al. (2006: 268) describe a similar phenomenon in their survey of prostitution-related articles that appeared in Victoria's daily newspaper, the *Times-Colonist*, between 1980 and 2005. They note that prostitutes were routinely produced as cunning criminals believed to "take pride in circumventing the law and avoiding arrest." In Canada, of course, the association of prostitution with criminality is exacerbated by the legal regimes that criminalize practices related to selling sex, as I describe in Chapter Two. Further, Lowman (2000: 1004) contends that the "outlaw status" of prostitution has had devastating implications for sex workers. By defining prostitutes as criminals, he argues, the law has reproduced an ideological context where "a woman working the street is particularly vulnerable to predatory misogynist violence" (Lowman 2000: 1004). Importantly, the illicit nature of prostitution in Canada forces the industry underground, a phenomenon that reaffirms both its actual and imagined connections to various forms of criminal activity.

Yet the sex worker's status as a symbol of danger is not simply a function of her presumed connection to criminality. Perhaps more important is the widespread perception that sex workers are vectors of disease. This is particularly true in Vancouver, where the Downtown Eastside was deemed the centre of an HIV epidemic in 1997. Intravenous drug use and sex work were seen as central factors in the outbreak, a perception that marked street-level prostitutes as a decidedly dangerous population. The association of disease with danger has been particularly pronounced with HIV. As Jean Comaroff (2007: 197–204) has noted, the virus has come to be seen as a "quintessential sign of all that imperils a civilized future-in-the-world, an iconic social pathology." The persistent conflation of sex work with the dangers of disease has the effect of "marking out pathologized publics" and "crystallizing latent… anxieties." As Ericson et al. (1991: 5) have argued, symbols are central to ordering "collective views of the world." The symbol of the prostitute has long contributed to such orderings, by providing an archetypal negative against which the norms of civilized citizenship might be contrasted and distinguished.

Sex workers have also been represented as potent symbols of moral corruption. The degree to which such characterizations have been sustained and reproduced in media narratives offers a compelling illustration of the news media's capacity to "participate in the constitution of moral boundaries of the society" in which they report (Ericson et al. 1987: 60). For much of the twentieth century, prostitutes were branded by press narratives as fallen women; imagined, that is, as individuals who had strayed from the norms of acceptable femininity and descended into a rank world of festering immorality and licentiousness. This has been particularly true of street-level workers, whose "corruption" was plainly visible to the public gaze. For Hubbard (1999: 77) this "visible eroticization of the public realm" came to represent the "most significant affront to a modern, patriarchal society in which women were considered as best confined to the sanctity of the feminized domestic space."

Even as patriarchal notions of acceptable female behaviour have transformed, some argue that the exchange of sex for commercial gain has remained a potent symbol of moral degeneracy. Press narratives in the United Kingdom have persistently branded sex workers and clients as "morally degenerate" precisely because of their "willingness to reduce sex to commercial exchange" (O'Neill et al. 2008: 76). For Hubbard (1999), the repudiation of this commercial sexuality is bound up in a desire to preserve certain heterosexist norms. He argues that contemporary views of prostitution as immoral often reflect the view that "woman's sexuality should only be expressed or available within the confines of a domesticated and reproductive relationship" (Hubbard 1999: 2). As such, the visible immorality of public prostitution has come to be seen as an affront to the enjoyment of city spaces by the mainstream public. A 1981 editorial in the *Times Colonist* captures this condemnatory spirit succinctly:

> Whores... not only offend... the law, they are an embarrassment when the family goes downtown for dinner. They speak of the community's failure. They are also seen as a threat by some wives and mothers and they are bad for business. (quoted in Hallgrimsdotir et al. 2006: 279)

This assessment offers a striking example of the ways in which street-involved women have been contrasted against (and seen as antithetical to) conventional female subjectivities.

The assumed danger of the prostitute's immorality — her capacity to bring corruption into the sphere of morally upright men and women — both contrasts her against and marks her as a threat to the valorized figures of mother and daughter. For Jiwani and Young (2006: 900), such characterizations have had important implications. In their survey of the *Vancouver Sun's* coverage of the case of the missing and murdered women, they note that this binary demarcates those "bodies that can and should be saved from those that are considered beyond redemption." Traditionally virtuous women (mothers, daughters, wives) are set up in sharp contrast to the "runaways" and "throwaways" mired in the corruption of street-level commercial sex. As we shall see, this contrast is powerfully reproduced in journalistic attempts to restore a certain dignity to the missing and murdered women by celebrating their status as family members and contrasting that against the immoral practices of sex work and narcotic use.

Representing the Prostitute

The coverage produces a relatively coherent if uncomplicated image of the prostitute. Each of the three newspapers, with notable consistency, mobilizes a series of recurring themes to explain this figure. They offer compelling ways to understand who it is that enters the industry and what it is that motivates her sustained participation. With little disruption, she is portrayed as a woman powerfully consumed by addiction, constantly at risk of predation and violence, yet undeterred by (or oblivious to) the constant peril of her work. Her presence on the stroll is frequently explained by reference to previous victimization, a foundational personal tragedy narrative that preceded her descent. Such personal histories explain the terror of the street as only the most recent in a series of abuses. Her connection to the illicit drug trade and the "outlaw status" of her work, meanwhile, mark her as part of a deviant and criminal underworld, a member of that illicit class that reproduces chaos in the inner city. Moreover, as I explain in the following chapter, she is produced as intractably linked to the degenerate space in which she works. By virtue of this association, she is subjected to the same "unremitting stigmatization" as the neighbourhood itself (Pratt 2005: 1062). These themes are reproduced in the substantive textual explanations that suffuse both the articles and the visual culture of the coverage — particularly in the prominent photographs and headlines that act as "cognitive organizers" — to further embed this dominant portrayal (Jiwani and Young 2006: 904).

While prostitution itself is a constant theme in the coverage, the image of the sex worker is primarily shaped through a group of eighteen articles and profiles that attempt to provide some substantive information about the people who enter the street-level industry. The majority of these articles (thirteen) are profiles of the six women that Pickton would eventually be convicted of murdering; the others (five) are more general stories about women currently working in street-level prostitution.

The victim profiles are marked by two somewhat contradictory patterns. In one sense, they attempt to overcome the powerful brandings of prostitute and addict by highlighting some of the more banal aspects of the women's lives and personalities. Here, the women are memorialized diversely: one as a poet and artist, another as a loyal friend and another as someone who loved the colour pink, for example. Such descriptions attempt to transcend stigmatization by positioning each victim as a subject who was more than part of a deviant underclass. But they also attempt to invest each victim with a personal history that extends beyond her experiences in the Downtown Eastside. Accordingly, these articles are the central vehicles through which each woman's tragic personal history is described; they attempt to bring her foundational descent into plain view. Their central narrative function, however, is the production of each woman as a member of a family (a daughter, a mother, a sister) whose absence is mourned — an important consideration that I discuss at length below.

In another sense, however, these profiles also operate to powerfully consolidate the victims as members of a deviant class. Themes of addiction, disease, survival sex and violence are central to these ostensibly sympathetic profiles. Their attempts to memorialize respectfully, usually by highlighting each woman's proximity to commonsense notions of respectability, are tempered by persistent allusions to her deviance. In one profile, Serena Abotsway is remembered as a "bubbly kind-hearted woman … [who] was an intravenous drug user and a prostitute" (*Globe and Mail* 2007a). Georgina Papin is remembered as a woman who "dressed nicely and smoked crack cocaine before going to work as a prostitute." Andrea Joesbury is remembered as a "polite, quiet woman... [who] was in a methadone program when she disappeared" (*Globe and Mail* 2007a). In each of these paradigmatic examples, narrations of conventional decency are countered by blunt reminders of a prevailing degeneracy.

These victim profiles, however, are far more balanced than the five articles that describe sex workers currently working in the industry. With varying degrees of sensationalism, this latter group of articles produces a strikingly narrow image of the street-involved woman. She is defined as an archetypically itinerant and irresponsible individual; divested of all context, she is produced as one-dimensional in her addiction, concerned only with the atavistic pursuit of her next fix. Importantly, descriptions of current workers are inflected by a persistent (if sometimes only suggestive) pattern of comparison that marks them as one and the same with the disappeared. In many places this conflation is unmistakable. Current workers are produced as the fortunate ones who, as one reporter puts it, "survived the era of a serial killer [only to] continue to risk it all... beatings, rape, disease" (DiManno 2007a). The textual production of the prostitute does not occur in isolation; it is imbedded in a visual culture that bolsters the themes outlined above. Headlines and sub-headlines are central to this process; they provide key messages — "cognitive organizers" — that orient the reader's interpretation by setting the tone of the news page and establishing what information is relevant (Van Dijk 1993; Jiwani and Young 2006: 904). Certain salient terms recur in these titles and reinforce themes of deviance. For example, the terms "prostitute," "hooker," "sex worker" and "sex trade worker" appear in twelve headlines and sub-headlines while the terms "addiction," "junkies" and "drugs," appear in eight. To put these figures in context, the words "missing" or "missing women" appear twentu-one times in the coverage. Prostitution is privileged in headlines roughly half as many times as disappearance, and narcotic dependency is emphasized in roughly one third as many. Yet the headline culture is as interesting in what it omits as what it implies. In spite of the dire economic circumstances that many of the missing and murdered women (as well those currently selling sex in the Downtown Eastside) are said to endure, there is not a single reference to economic marginalization in any of the headlines or sub-headlines; the term "poverty," for example, does not appear in a single title. Moreover, in spite of the striking overrepresentation of Aboriginal women among the missing and murdered, only one reference to Aboriginality appears in the headlines, a disturbing elision that signals the coverage's prevailing unwillingness to interrogate this trend.

The cohesiveness of the image of the prostitute is further accomplished by the photographic culture of the coverage. In total, twenty-nine images of street-involved women appear in three coverage periods. Of these, twenty-four are photographs (or groups of photographs) of the missing and murdered women themselves while the other five are of women that are presently street-involved. Of this first group, twenty-one are composed of mug-shot style images, all of which appeared on the official missing women posters produced by civic authorities, a link that, as Jiwani and Young (2006: 898) observe, "reinforce[s] ... the women's association with criminality." These line-ups saturate the coverage, appearing at least once on the front page of all three newspapers. They are unflattering, close cropped and conjure associations with familiar prisoner processing photographs. Clustered together as they so often are, these mug-shot collages collapse distinctions between individuals, producing the collective as a common caste, those who experienced a shared destiny born of a shared lifestyle.

While the photographs of the missing and murdered women suggest deviance largely through association, the five photographs of currently street-involved women establish the connection directly. These arresting images feature women injecting heroin, smoking crack, soliciting clients, sitting glassy-eyed on a dirty sidewalk and loitering on an industrial loading bay. On their own, they have a dramatic effect, signalling the radical distance of their subjects from conventional norms of safety and purity. Simultaneously, they invest textual accounts of deviance with the authority of graphic proof. And their significance is further amplified by the headlines that accompany them. One image appears beneath the headline "Can't get lower than this" while another appears above the title "Always on edge" (Hutchinson 2007). Another makes the link between those currently on the street and the disappeared unmistakable: a lurid shot of a woman injecting narcotics into her neck appears alongside the headline "I guess I'm lucky to be alive" (Girard 2002b).

Accredited Sources and Authoritative Statements

Within professional cultures of news production, accounts of observed reality are expected to be grounded in (or corroborated by) the "authoritative statements" of "accredited sources" (Hall et al. 1978: 58). Such practices are central to preserving the news organization's reputation as a disinterested and impartial observer. Outside evidence from established authorities is employed to confer a sense of objectivity and universality on the otherwise subjective accounts of individual journalists. As some have observed, such practices have had the important effect of providing certain individuals and organizations with systematic "over-accessing" to the media (Hall et al. 1978: 58). Others have observed that news discourses do not merely mediate information about particular events through institutional authority, they also provide "knowledge about who are the key power holders, the 'authorized knowers' in the knowledge society" (Ericson et al. 1987: 18).

The case of the missing and murdered women provides compelling evidence of institutional over-representation. Authoritative claims from representatives of police departments, government bureaucracies and various sites of established institutional power are an important feature of the coverage and serve as a key means of advancing particular narrations. When considering how the coverage has produced particular images of the prostitute, however, such institutional know-ers are hardly the most relevant contributors. Information about sex workers is largely drawn from three other sources: the families and friends of the missing and murdered women, advocates and allies of street-involved women, and sex workers themselves.

In spite of this reduced reliance on institutional authority, we might still observe a distinct "hierarchy of credibility" between these source groups; their contributions provide distinct evidence of a sustained "over-accessing" of par-ticular groups (Hall et al. 1978). The family and friends of the missing and mur-dered women were quoted 109 times in the coverage, roughly five and half times more than advocates and allies of street involved women (quoted twenty times) and roughly eleven times more than sex workers themselves (quoted ten times). Accordingly, questions of how the image of the prostitute is produced in the cover-age must also be questions of who is authorized to contribute to that production.

The Representational Authority of Family and Friends

Statements attributed to the family and friends of missing and murdered women provide the most comprehensive source of information about sex workers operat-ing in the Downtown Eastside. These statements are central to the construction of the prevailing definitions of the prostitute that emerge from the coverage. Taken together, these 109 quotations accomplish several core narrative functions. They are employed to advance the narrative of the investigation by demonstrating how personal grief intersects with each procedural development. They are also frequently invoked to explain frustration with the police handling of the case, as I explain in Chapter Two. For present purposes, however, it is useful to focus on two other narrative contributions that this group provides. First, they are a key source of information about how each woman ended up in the Downtown Eastside's street-level sex trade. Second, they provide personal and even idiosyncratic details about the individual victims, anecdotal proof that the missing and murdered women were "more than drug addicted prostitutes," as one prominent headline puts it (Armstrong and Matas 2007).

Family and friends are the primary source of biographical information about the missing and murdered women. They are mobilized to explain each victim's apparent fall from grace, those circumstances which explain her involvement in the sinister world of the innercity street. While there is significant variation in the specific content of each story, there is also a discernable common denominator between them. Each provides a personal tragedy narrative that renders the victim's presence in the Downtown Eastside understandable. A distinct pattern emerges from these narratives. Behind each of the murdered women is a history of victim-ization, a series of individualized abuses that both precede and are said to have caused her turn to narcotic dependency and survival sex.

Biographical sketches of the victims are suffused with accounts of parental addiction, fetal alcohol syndrome, racism, sexual and physical abuse, predatory foster parents and exploitative boyfriends. These early trauma are privileged as the decisive foundations of a life of victimization. Of the twenty articles that provide biographical sketches of the victims, twelve invoke family members and friends to attest to these foundational tragedies. Consider the following examples taken from each of the three newspapers:

(i) It was a sad existence that could be traced to her early childhood. Her father died in her arms when she was 3. Separated from her mother and seven other siblings, she was put in foster homes that, according to her brother, "left a lot to be desired."

The first foster home was "a nightmare" in which she was physically abused and subjected to sever mental torture. (Armstrong and Matas 2007)

(ii) Ms. Papin had a troubled life growing up in Alberta, bouncing from foster homes to group homes to residential schools. She began experimenting with drugs at age 11, her brother Rick Papin said in an interview in 2001. (*National Post* 2007a)

(iii) The naïve teen ran away from a difficult childhood on Vancouver Island to Vancouver's Downtown Eastside to pursue her dream of finding a husband and having a baby.

"She found this guy and she fell in love with him," her grandfather Jack Cummer said.

"Eventually she phoned and let me know he was 15 or 20 years older than she was, so it gave her two things: A man she loved and a father figure. But she was put on the streets because he was a drug dealer." (*National Post* 2007a)

(iv) Sarah deVries was also troubled. Growing up as a black child in a white neighborhood in the 1970s, she was teased and subjected to racist taunts. At home, while her older siblings and parents could sympathize, they could not relate.

"It was really tough for her growing up with nobody who shared her experience on that fundamental level" said Maggie deVries, a children's book author and editor.

When Sarah was 9 her parents split up. As the youngest, she took it hard. By her teens, she was in with the wrong crowd, using drugs, running away and frequenting the streets. It's unclear whether she completed Grade 8. By age 17, she was gone for good. (Girard 2002c)

(v) He [Sereena Abotsway's foster father] said she was severely abused before she arrived at the Draayers, adding that he couldn't elaborate because the person who inflicted the harm is still alive. "Sereena was definitely damaged" he said. She lived with the Draayers until age 17 and called them Mom and Dad. (Armstrong and Matas 2007)

These examples are representative of a larger narrative trend that establishes the missing and murdered women as traumatized and damaged subjects, driven to addiction and survival sex by individualized patterns of abuse. Importantly, these stories help to memorialize the slain. They remind audiences that the victims were not merely the haphazardly chosen prey of a deranged individual, but persons who had experienced a continuum of brutal violence. Yet this privileging of foundational abuse operates to individualize each tragedy. It privatizes suffering and obscures the role of larger structural forces in reproducing and sustaining the dangers that each woman confronted.

Secondly, statements attributed to family members and friends are central to journalistic efforts to transcend the stigmas of prostitute and addict. They operate to reinvest the victims with a sense of conventional respectability. They demonstrate that the women were more than merely street-involved; they were "real people with real stories" (Armstrong and Matas 2007). In each of the sources there is a declared effort to restore a certain degree of normalcy to the victims. Central to this effort is an attempt to demonstrate that each of the victims cultivated conventional family relationships. Friends and family members are important here; as mourning loved ones, they provide potent proof of these conventional bonds and as quoted sources they provide credible biographical information that illustrates their veracity. Beneath headlines like "Sister was a prostitute but so much more" (Matas 2002b), "Little sister behind the statistic" (Girard 2002b), "These are our sisters, our daughters, our mothers" (*National Post* 2007a), friends and family are invoked to demonstrate, as one *Toronto Star* correspondent would have it, that the victims were "not just drug addicts and whores but daughters, wives, mothers, human beings" (DiManno 2007b).

Their statements are used to juxtapose the deviant practices of narcotic use and prostitution with the apparently real and human practices of being a mother, a daughter or a wife. Numerous quotations attributed to Rick Frey, father of the murdered Marnie Frey, (perhaps inadvertently) establish this binary even as he attempts to restore a positive "public perception" of the victims. As he puts it: "the Downtown Eastside women were portrayed as being prostitutes, hookers, drug addicts. They weren't — they were our daughters, our sisters, our mothers." And elsewhere: "[these] are our sisters, our daughters, our mothers — all human beings" (*National Post* 2007b). Similarly, Maggie DeVries is repeatedly invoked, insisting that the missing and murdered women were "real people" with real family connections. The *Globe and Mail*'s Robert Matas (2002b) writes:

The family of one of Vancouver's missing prostitutes is concerned that the women will be perceived as one-dimensional caricatures similar to the characters in movies about prostitution and murder.

Maggie deVries said yesterday that she wants the missing women remembered as people with lives and families.

"It's for real," she said in an interview. "They were real people."

Elsewhere in the coverage, Greg Garley, foster brother of Mona Wilson, memorializes his murdered sister in equally familial terms: "I remember what a great girl she was. She would have made a great mother" (*Toronto Star* 2007b). Elsewhere again, in a set of victim profiles, and beneath the heading, "Tried to get clean," Brenda Wolfe is commemorated in similar tones (*Globe and Mail* 2007a). Here, a quotation attributed to a friend that Wolfe met in a substance-abuse program reads: "I will always remember her smile and the beautiful son she had while in recovery" (*Globe and Mail* 2007a). In one sense, the examples above, and the numerous others like them, represent a genuine effort to restore dignity to a group of relentlessly stigmatized women. Yet in another sense, they operate to entrench a binary between the presumed authenticity and innate humanness of traditional familial roles (mother, daughter, sister) on the one hand, and the sub-humanity of street-involvement on the other. They imply that the normalized practices of family life are what was "real" and "human" about each victim. I return to this theme again below.

The Representational Authority of Advocates and Allies

What I refer to as the advocates and allies of sex workers here are those who either work directly with people in the Downtown Eastside — community organization service providers, for example — and others who, in their own capacity, advocate for policy reform or institutional change that would make the practices of street-level sex work less dangerous. As such, this group is uniquely positioned to provide two kinds of contributions to the coverage. Those who work with sex workers in the neighbourhood are able to offer information about the experience of street involvement, contributions that contrast with those of family members who were primarily called upon to provide information about the woman before they began working in the Downtown Eastside. Community workers are called upon to provide information about what is happening, or what had been happening, at the street level itself. Moreover, those who advocate for changes to the regulatory status quo — critical academics and sympathetic politicians, for example — are primarily enlisted in the coverage to bolster criticisms of the police or the state more generally.

With these considerations in mind, we might expect the most compelling critiques of the prevailing stigmatizations of the prostitute to come from this group. As individuals who work closely with street-involved women, community workers are well positioned to challenge stereotypical characterizations. Similarly, as individuals who study prostitution or are involved in the construction of public policy, other allies are well positioned to provide potent critiques of current conditions and they have the credentials necessary to be considered authorities in the mainstream press. It is from this group that some of the most robust critiques of the status quo are launched but they account for a very small number of quotations and contributions. In 156 articles examined, only twenty statements come from this group and many appeared in the same articles. As such, their significance must be weighed against the much broader themes that define the coverage. The placement and context of these iterations ensured that even contributions that might be called critical were primarily employed to bolster dominant definitions of the prostitute.

As individuals with daily exposure to street-involved women, community workers and allies are in a position to provide essential context for journalistic accounts of street involvement; their institutional affiliation marks them as credible sources. Predictably, their contributions tend to appear in the articles that attempt to provide some analysis of working conditions in the Downtown Eastside. Numerous accounts draw on Elaine Allan, a coordinator with Women in Need of a Safe House (WISH), a Downtown Eastside drop-in centre, to provide a sense of what life is like on the neighbourhood's low-track strolls. Explanations attributed to her offer a portrait of the sex worker as an individual whose basic judgment has been catastrophically impaired by addiction. Allan describes a constant physical struggle frequently misunderstood by those outside of it. As she puts it in one article:

> These women are just so addicted. Maybe people from mainstream society think it's just a big party down there every night and these women should just pull themselves up by their bootstraps. Believe me it's no party. (DiManno 2007c)

Elsewhere, Allan is called upon to describe the experience of addiction in more detail:

> Elaine Allan, who once worked at a Vancouver drop-in centre for prostitutes, knew five of the six women. Ms. Allan said drug addiction, in its final stages, robs people of their personalities.
> "The reality of it is that addicted women are lonely and they're vulnerable and they're isolated and they're afraid and they get beaten up a lot. Once you're here, there's no way out." (Armstrong and Matas 2007)

Jamie Lee Hamilton, another neighbourhood advocate, also emphasizes the power of addiction. As she puts it:

Everyone out there is in survival mode … it's hard to focus on your safety when more pressing needs are getting the next fix, affording food, finding a place to stay and making sure a shameless pimp is paid off. (Girard 2002b)

Unlike other narratives about the missing women that tend to consider addiction in less contextualized ways, the explanations provided by advocates and allies offer important considerations of the multiple oppressions that street-involved women often shoulder. Taken together, they offer compelling accounts of survival sex as an ongoing experience of victimization. Allan describes women who are not only burdened by powerful narcotic dependencies but also haunted by poverty, inadequate police protection and an ever-present threat of violence. Her contributions disrupt, to some degree, narratives that suggest street involvement is a kind of self-selected deviance, an actively willed alternative lifestyle. As she puts it:

I know that a lot of these women come from horrific situations at home, from foster care. They've been physically and sexually abused. But there's no haven on the streets. This is where the real abuse happens. (DiManno 2007c)

This sentiment is echoed elsewhere by another WISH coordinator, Kate Gibson. Describing concerns that media narratives might reproduce certain stereotypical impressions, she notes:

There's a huge stigma attached to being a sex-trade worker … [w]e don't want them to be further stigmatized by the media. It's hard to tell their stories fairly because there are just so many reasons why they've ended up here. It's about poverty and isolation and abuse and addiction. (DiManno 2007a)

These examples are representative of the larger role that advocates and allies play in representing the experience of street involvement.

Taken together, this group's contributions provide an important disruption of the generally facile interpretations of prostitution that the coverage provides. Nevertheless, they are limited in two important ways. First, in spite of their relatively unique attempts to consider prostitution as something more than a self-selected lifestyle, they do, in many ways, contribute to a larger narrative pattern that individualizes the terror of the stroll. They tend to emphasize the connection between personal histories of abuse and addiction and marginalization. While such contributions are important, and certainly not inaccurate, they have the inadvertent effect of obscuring, and in some cases even eliding, other oppressive forces that shape particular kinds of marginality.

Secondly, they are limited by their location in the coverage. All of these contributions appear as anomalous disruptions in articles that profoundly emphasize deviance, criminality, licentiousness and crazed addiction. As such, their capacity to re-imagine the prostitute is powerfully tempered by a more prominent textual and visual culture that aggressively inscribes simple understandings of this figure as a deviant other and a subject with dubious morality.

It is important to note that other advocates and allies do provide some of the most potent criticisms of the sex workers' relationship with the police and the state more generally. Several credentialed researchers and politicians provide incisive critiques. The most significant of these "authorized knowers" is Lowman, a renowned criminologist with a well-established history of challenging official approaches to sex work. He is invoked in five articles and in each of the newspapers. As the investigation began to unfold, Lowman provided the most scathing criticisms of the official response to the crisis. In one article, for example, he denounces the notion that sex workers are the "authors of their own misfortune" and chastises police for the selectivity of their protection (Girard 2002e). Elsewhere he argues:

> If 50 women in any other category, whether housewives, women of a certain age or anyone else, went missing, believe me, the police reaction would have been entirely different. (Matas 2002a)

Others made similar statements. Provincial Member of the Legislative Assembly Jenny Kwan, for example, told the *Toronto Star*: "you have to question why the investigation wasn't taken seriously earlier… these are real people who are somebody's daughter or granddaughter. We have to show their lives are worth something" (Girard 2002e).

To a much lesser degree, advocates and allies were able to broaden the notion of victimization by implicating the state in a critique that extended beyond a mere denunciation of police inaction. To take one unfortunately uncommon example, Harsha Walia, a coordinator with the Downtown Eastside Women's Centre, was able to connect victimization with growing poverty, declining social assistance and inadequate housing. In perhaps the most important critique in the entire body of coverage, Walia was able to provide a compelling account of some of the structural forces that have reproduced the marginality of street-involved women. Hume's (2007) *Globe and Mail* article reads:

> Ms. Walia says the answer to making the streets safer for women lies in addressing the root causes. She notes, for example, that under provincial regulations a single mother who has been getting social assistance will lose that support once her child turns three.
> "That's why a lot of single moms who can't find work and can't afford child care end up turning tricks on the street.
> "It's good Pickton has been convicted, but all these things — housing, poverty, child apprehension, social assistance regulations — all of those issues are making it just a lot more dangerous for women," she said.

Walia's contribution provides an unprecedented account of how structural forces have come to bear on street-involved women. It disrupts dominant renderings of the sex worker as a deviant addict and illuminates how structural inequality has, in fact, actively produced these subjects. Her critique, however, is unique in the coverage. It is a rare contribution that disrupts the facile production of the prostitute as a degenerate subject, a branding which otherwise saturates the coverage.

The Self-Representational Work of Sex Workers

Current and former sex workers play a decidedly peripheral role in the coverage and are quoted a mere ten times in its entirety. Prostitutes themselves have little say in the process of their own representation. They are not authorized in any substantive way to construct knowledge about their lives. This process is left to others. Yet it is not merely the small number of quotations that ensure this erasure, it is also their content. Statements attributed to currently street-involved sex workers privilege a single and nearly univocal set of meanings. They construct and consolidate the image of the prostitute as an oblivious woman consumed by a one-dimensional drive for narcotics. Consider the following examples:

(i) Josey is a 34-year-old prostitute with scabs all over face, the result, she said, of a bad batch of cocaine cut with Ajax. She saw the news about the farm on TV, but hadn't talked to anyone about it.

"I just came out now," she explained, as she wandered over to a friend who supplies pipes. Crack pipes, that is, which Josey hawks on the corner for $2 a pop.

Josey said she and a few girlfriends were sitting around last week, wondering what happened to the bodies of the missing women. "Fifty girls missing and no bodies. Kind of strange."

"When I heard on the news about the farm, man, it sent a cold chill down my spine."

Josey knew many of the missing, most of them casually, one intimately. "We had just started dating," Josey, who is bisexual, said. "She went out one night and never came back." (Gill 2002)

(ii) Suarez who uses the street name, "Brown Sugar," said she's been selling sex on Vancouver's streets since she was 14 and knew about half of the missing women.

"I guess I'm lucky to be alive," she said before wandering down the street to buy a rock of crack cocaine, which will take the edge off for half an hour. (Girard 2002b)

(iii) Toronto native Shelley Creor, who has sold her body for 11 years on the area's streets to support a four-hit-per-day heroin habit, said she has little hope that an arrest in the case would help ease the violence faced by her and other prostitutes on a daily basis.

"Nobody cares for anybody but themselves," said Creor, 38, before wandering down an alleyway for a fix, injected into her throat by using the mirror of a parked van to locate the right spot. She was soon gone in search of a $40 trick to pay for the next hit. (Girard 2002b)

(iv) "Can't get any lower than this," snorts Pauline, a crack addict whose still pretty face belies the fact that she's worked as a prostitute for 21 years, sometimes uptown, sometimes downtown, from escort agency to curbside. "When all you care about is where your next toke is coming from, you'll do the sex for just the drugs, forget the money." (DiManno 2007a)

(v) "Sure, I remember those women," says Pauline, 39 ... "For years there was talk on the street of parties and pig roasts out at some farm. Some of us didn't like the idea of going so far out of the city. Or maybe I just wasn't desperate enough back then. Then the girls started disappearing.

"But the truth is, we never looked that hard at what was happening. When you're an addict, you don't care about other people's problems, you're not even aware of what's happening outside yourself. Down here, it's Independence Day, 24 hours a day." (DiManno 2007a)

There is an arresting harmony between these quotations. Taken together, they create a singular portrait. The prostitute is produced as an abject other; a one- dimensional figure, incapable of inter-personal solidarity and concerned only with her next fix. She is never invited to comment on the conditions of her daily life. Neither is she offered the opportunity to consider what might make that life less dangerous or more tolerable. It is at worst assumed — and at best it is implied — that narcotic dependency is the causal condition of her presence on the stroll. Nowhere is it considered that addiction might well have emerged as a response to brutality, as a numbing agent to the horrors of marginality. Interestingly, however, the source of these quotations engenders them with a certain gravitas. Their irrefutability is established precisely because they come from sex workers themselves. As Smart has observed, audiences tend to be compelled by personal testimony; as she puts it, "personal testimony is given the status of truth" (quoted in Van Brunschot et al. 1999: 50).

The Dominant Paradigm

When we consider what has been said about the prostitute — and perhaps more importantly, who has been authorized to say it, we find that these descriptions coalesce around a relatively coherent and unified image. They not only offer compelling ways to understand who the missing and murdered women were but also a framework for understanding the lives of street-involved women more generally, including those currently working the strolls of the Downtown Eastside.

Other studies that have considered how the crisis has been taken up by news discourses have also observed that the figure of the prostitute was produced through a tightly limited set of categories. Jiwani and Young (2006) observe that news narratives operated to "frame" the missing and murdered women in ways that emphasized their status as addicts and prostitutes while highlighting the Aboriginal heritage of some of the women. Geraldine Pratt (2005: 1062) argues that in the "imaginative geographies" of popular representations of the spaces of prostitution, sex workers "continue to be represented almost exclusively as diseased, criminalized, impoverished and degenerate bodies."

The coverage yields compelling evidence of the persistence of these same characterizations. Yet perhaps sensitive to the charge that the mass media has been complicit in caricaturizing, stigmatizing and even demonizing street-level sex workers in the past, the coverage studied here is marked by an effort to both memorialize and represent prostitutes less dismissively. One of the *Toronto Star's* first reports on the case noted that "the women's loved ones are determined to attach names, faces and stories to people often ignored because they exist on society's fringe" (Girard 2002a). Importantly, coverage in each of the sources seems to reflect a similar determination. This effort takes shape in the attempts to provide background and biographical information about the six women whose murders were being prosecuted. Each paper's supposed commitment to respectful coverage is enunciated by the sustained iteration of sanctimonious reminders that the slain were "real people."

Yet in spite of efforts to restore a degree of dignity to the murdered, the above analysis demonstrates that in its totality the coverage operates to perpetuate a limited set of dominant definitions. It re-inscribes many of the problematic characterizations described by Pratt, Jiwani and Young. By privileging narcotic dependency and foundational tragedy as the core explanations for the sex worker's presence on the low-track stroll, the coverage effectively occludes the possibility of interrogating the role of structural factors in reproducing marginality and driving women into the precarious universe of survival sex. Given the limited say that sex workers are afforded in the construction of knowledge about their lives, however, such erasures are not entirely surprising. Brock (1998: 11) has noted that at points where prostitution has been constituted as a "social problem," sex workers themselves have frequently been excluded from suggesting solutions for its resolution. Defining sex workers as "the problem" has had the effect of keeping them "outside of the debate, silenced by groupings that can claim a more legitimate interest." Yet, as she insists, "without the contributions of those who work in prostitution, there can be no resolution" (Brock 1998: 11).

As I demonstrate above, however, the input of sex workers is not entirely absent from the coverage. Rather, they provide some limited information, contributions that seem to be constrained by either the questions asked or the story told. These narrow contributions create the potent illusion of balanced journalism. That is, they seem to evidence that reporters have done the hard work of consulting all relevant parties in the construction of their narratives. In fact, one journalist writes with a righteous insistence of the importance of speaking to sex workers, condemning those who would try to shield street-involved women from the hazards of exploit-ative journalism:

> Advocates warned reporters not to exploit the sex workers on the Eastside, as if giving them the opportunity to talk about their lives was an untoward invasion of privacy. The language police scrutinize stories lest unaccept-able descriptors be applied to the sad souls who lurch about Skid Row in drug-induced stupor. We're all admonished about "sensitivity" and value-neutral observations. But this isn't a morality play. It's harsh reality, the sleazy underbelly of a beautiful cosmopolitan city. It does no good to turn away or smooth out the rough, ugly details. In fact, it does harm — one more way of not looking, not seeing. (DiManno 2007b)

DiManno makes a compelling claim. She suggests that engaging street-involved women is central to a process of making them visible. As David Sibley (1995: 29) observes, drawing on bell hooks' notion of "repositioning," "engaging with the other... might lead to understanding, [and to] a rejection of a stereotype and a lesser concern with threats to the boundaries of the community." Yet for Sibley, any such engagement harbours an implicit danger. He writes:

> Any optimism about such a move should be tempered with the thought that limited engagement, a superficial encounter, might result in the pre-sumption of knowledge which could be more damaging than ignorance. (Sibley 1995: 29)

It seems to me that the dominant images of the prostitute that emerge from the coverage provide precisely such a "superficial encounter." Through their reliance on particular kinds of sources, their preference for particular aspects of life in the Downtown Eastside, and their profound inattention to structural violence, jour-nalistic representations of sex workers both presume and reproduce a knowledge that does more harm than good. In particular, there are problematic ramifications of contrasting sex workers with the valorized feminine roles of the conventional family, limits to the personal tragedy narrative as an explanation for street-involvement and inherent dangers in the sustained reproduction of sex workers as a deviant and criminal population.

The persistent contrasting of sex work with conventional female domesticity has important ideological implications. In the first place, it imagines an unbridgeable gulf between the sex worker, on the one hand, and the mother, the daughter, the sister and the wife, on the other. The former connotes corruption and immorality while the latter connotes a series of celebrated, morally sound modes of femininity. Accordingly, the coverage is marked by a profound effort to distance the murdered from the former category by reminding audiences of their affinity to the latter. Crucially, it is the categories of domestic value that are the primary rhetorical weapons of the journalistic attempt to restore a certain dignity to the slain.

The (perhaps inadvertent) effects of these attempts at sympathetic portrayal are profound. First, they position the practices of prostitution on the nefarious side of a Manichean divide. The repeated reminders that, in spite of their presence in the Downtown Eastside, the victims were also valued members of families, reinforces a perceived distance between the morality of the family space and the immorality of the spaces of prostitution. Jiwani and Young (2006: 904) argue that descriptions of the missing and murdered women as members of families makes them more like "us." As they put it: "it rescues them from a place of degeneracy to a zone of normality." Yet such positioning does more than merely redeem the stigmatized. For Jiwani and Young (2006: 904):

> it conforms to the dominant hegemonic values, in that the only women who can be rescued or are worth saving are mothers, daughters, and sisters — women like us. Making them like "us" is a discursive move designed to privilege their deservedness both in terms of police intervention and social recognition.

Thus importantly, the sex worker's degree of belonging to conventional familial structures becomes a primary determinant of her value. The implication of such constructions is that those who cannot be seen as part of the imagined "us" are irredeemable

The coverage's privileging of personal tragedy narratives is also of central ideological importance. In one sense, it allows audiences to understand the street-involved as marginalized people, as the victims of profound personal tragedy. As Cohen (2002: 7) has observed, "each society possesses a set of ideas about what causes deviation… and a set of images of who constitutes the typical deviant;" information, he contends, which arrives "already processed by the mass media." For our purposes here, it is useful to consider how ideas about what causes deviation are reproduced and processed by the coverage. Here, individualized personal tragedies are mobilized as the core explanations for the deviant turn of the sex worker and a distinct "set of images" — predatory boyfriends, abusive parents, neglect, domestic instability — provide compelling evidence of their veracity. As such, their status as "victims" is constrained by the particular boundaries of individualized devastation.

The suggestion that foundational personal tragedy explains how individuals become involved in sex work jars against compelling comparative research that contrasts media narratives about what drives women to the strolls with the actual testimony of sex workers. For example, Hallgrimsdottir et al. (2003) note that media narratives tend to privilege forms of entrapment as the primary explanation for entry into prostitution, yet their research with sex workers cites a diverse "variety of circumstances" that motivated entry. They observe that:

> just over one third [of respondents] said that they became involved in the industry because they were enticed by a presenting opportunity, such as having peers who were involved, seeing an employment ad, or having someone approach them with an offer of money for sex. For over one quarter of respondents, however, economic duress — described as being "unable to find a job," "on welfare with small children," living "on the streets with no income" or having "bills to pay" — was the main motivating factor, and in many cases economic need overlapped with opportunity (Hallgrimsdottir et al. 2006: 276)

Benoit et al. did not consult exclusively with women working at the bottom of the street-level sex trade but their observations are nonetheless instructive here. They suggest that participation in prostitution is more complex than personal tragedy. The point here is not to deny or minimize the foundational atrocities suffered by many of the missing and murdered women; rather, it is to challenge the narrative closure that the coverage's privileging of these stories accomplishes. As I argue above, such narrations individualize tragedy and extricate broader complicities in the reproduction of dangerous conditions and the marginalization of particular people.

There is a pronounced coherence between these simplistic individualizing narratives and the ideological core that animates the politics of neoliberalism. Neoliberal notions of self-reliance valorize a strident individualism and position each individual as the master of her own well-being (see Chapter Two). Bourdieu (1998) describes the proliferation of this logic, as the "imposition everywhere... of that sort of moral Darwinism that institutes the struggle of all against all and cynicism as the norm of all action and behaviour." Individual devastation becomes entirely more understandable in a social and political milieu where the collective defenses against individual devastation have been powerfully undermined and dismantled. Thus for Zygmunt Baumann (2007: 14) the rise of a hegemonic neoliberalism produces a context where "it is now left to individuals to seek, find and practice individual solutions to socially produced troubles... while being equipped with tools and resources that are blatantly inadequate to the task." Following Baumann, we can see how the narrative characterization of survival sex as the product of an individual tragedy obscures the possibility of a broader analysis of marginalization. Of course, there are peripheral disruptions of this pattern in the coverage. On their own, however, they are hardly sufficient to undermine the prevailing messages of the whole, which install personal tragedy as the decisive explanation for the prostitutes' descent.

Finally, the persistent privileging of the relationship between sex work and criminal deviance reinforces the impression of a self-imposed (or even self-selected) marginality. The sustained deployment of images that signal the interconnection of prostitution and other threatening practices naturalizes the sex worker's presence in the inner city. Narcotic dependency is installed as the first principle of her existence. Her presence in the notorious spaces of the Downtown Eastside is naturalized. The criminal space and the criminal body are represented as interlocked in a mutually-constituting dialectic. Individuals are assumed to adhere to a certain set of deviant behaviors by virtue of the space they inhabit. The "association of prostitution with the drug trade as an almost natural, if not inevitable association, provides fuel for the contention that prostitution epitomizes the filth of the streets," a theme to which I return to in the following chapter. "Media reports do not investigate the claims that the conditions of the prostitute's life predispose them to drug use. Rather, drug use marks the prostitute as deviant" (Van Brunschot et al. 1999: 56). The coverage's striking emphasis on addiction and the lurid textual and visual representations of women injecting, smoking and exchanging drugs stresses their relationship to criminality.

As Hall et al. (1978: 225) observe, popular representations of deviance are frequently marked by processes of signification which imply the "convergence" of deviant practices that occurs when "two or more activities are linked in the process of signification so as to implicitly or explicitly draw parallels between them." The conflation of prostitution with illicit drug use is paradigmatic of this phenomenon. For Hall et al. (1978: 226), the representation of a "convergence" of practices that breach defined "thresholds" of public acceptance, escalate their unacceptability and make it easier for authorities to "mount legitimate campaigns of control against them." Yet, far more central to the purposes of this study, they observe that the representation of converging deviant practices has had the structural tendency of "translating a *political* issue in to a *criminal* one." The "solution" to the problem of deviant inner city phenomena is thus defined in terms of criminal enforcement rather than political change. The objective is thus conceived as one of policing criminal activity rather than addressing marginalization through progressive public policies. Hall et al. contend that such processes simplify complex issues by "transposing" analytic frameworks that "depoliticise [sic] ... an issue by *criminalising* [sic] it" [emphasis in original] (Hall et al. 1978: 229).

Thus, as we have seen, the coverage reproduces coherent ways of understanding the street-level prostitute. Through an over-reliance on two well-established discourses — the prostitute as part of a dangerous underworld and the prostitute and as an agent of moral corruption — it provides a distinct set of definitions that camouflage structural forms of violence. This elision hinges crucially on representational patterns that rely on particularly narrative authorities while silencing others. The relative absence of contributions from sex workers themselves necessarily limits the definitions that operate to reproduce the view that sex workers are in many ways the authors of their own misfortune.

Chapter 4

Producing Skid Row

*We can't sanitize the area or convince people it's pristine. We're looking for a
more youthful, risk-oblivious person... as soon as it's seen as the cool place to
be they'll be crawling over the bodies to get there.* — John Stovell, Vancouver
condo developer

they say 'we are swallowing up the Downtown Eastside
we will drive the low-life out
this is the day we wait for
to make our city a city for tourists and corporations
this is the day we work for
when we drive out the bad poor
and drive out their agencies
except for the good poor
who will live quietly and intimidated
in enclaves of social housing'
and our enemies gloat over how easy it is
to destroy our community
how easy it is
to divide our community
how easy it is — Bud Osborn, *Lamentation for the Downtown Eastside*

The characterization of Vancouver's Downtown Eastside as a space of urban
chaos suffuses the coverage studied. In each newspaper, a sustained deployment of provocative text and image operates to establish the neighbourhood as
a zone of illicit activity, omnipresent danger and a generalized degeneracy. Such
descriptions both infer and directly identify the area's disconnection from the relative safety of other city spaces. In effect, they produce the distinct impression of a
bifurcated city centre composed of two distinct worlds: one of order and civility,
the other of chaos.

Importantly, the emergence of the case of the missing and murdered women as
a national media spectacle does not mark the first time that this imagined division
has entered the "media mill." Since the 1980s, local and national news reports have
covered a series of dramatic events that have produced and sustained the neighbourhood's notorious reputation and reified its isolation from other parts of Vancouver's

prosperous urban core. Sommers and Blomley (2002), for example, argue that after local health officials identified the Downtown Eastside as the ground zero of an HIV epidemic in 1997, a moral panic erupted which fundamentally altered popular perceptions of the neighbourhood. They contend that "the elision of boundaries between differing categories of phenomena and the blurring of causes and effects," which is typical of such panics, had the effect of conflating drug use and sickness with the poverty that was already widespread and well known in the neighbourhood (Sommers and Blomley 2002: 21). Media reports were instrumental, they argue, in provoking a "pathologization of the poor" which soon turned into a "pathologization of the entire neighbourhood" (Sommers and Blomley 2002: 21).

Media treatment of the missing and murdered women cannot be considered outside of these well-established meanings. The reproduction of their stories does not occur in a geographical vacuum; each is indelibly marked by the traces of these previous iterations and the ways of seeing that they promote. The disappeared are produced not merely as sex workers, addicts or the victims of a predatory misogynist, but as women who lived their lives amidst a generalized chaos. Such accounts function as narrative vehicles of "territorial socialization" (Newman 2006: 87). They produce compelling ways to understand the crisis not merely in social and moral terms, but also in spatial terms.

In what follows, I demonstrate how the coverage works to map the Downtown Eastside; I argue that through a comprehensive diffusion of images of street-level chaos it operates to symbolically situate the neighbourhood as a distinct and disconnected urban segment. But this symbolic division has a material foundation. As we shall see, there are demonstrable linkages between the emergence of the Downtown Eastside as a space of concentrated "chaos" and the practices that have secured the ordered peace of the neighbourhoods that surround it. In spite of these connections, however, the coverage reproduces the imagined bifurcation of Vancouver through a sustained othering of the Downtown Eastside. In this, it creates an ideological absence with distinct material consequences; narrations that presume a prevailing inner city anarchy offer compelling ways to rationalize and justify the eviction of marginalized peoples from the increasingly valuable spaces of the city's central core.

War Is Peace: Two Parts of the Same City

Notions of an inner city space called "skid row" emerged in North American urban discourse in the decades that followed the Second World War. As Sommers (1998) observes, the broad range of social observers that described these recently discovered enclaves of poverty and social dislocation employed discursive strategies that mirrored earlier investigations of urban "slums." Their characterizations tended to forge "a causal nexus between the evident decay of the built environment and the supposedly dissolute character of its inhabitants." In contrast to the spaces of ordered civility, accounts of "skid row" produced the impression of a space that was "fundamentally backward." Vancouver was among the urban agglomerations where this phenomenon was being observed. Here, the shifting geographies of industrial activity and warehousing that had long been centred in the city's Downtown Eastside facilitated a shifting of spatial identifications. As industry fled the urban core, the Downtown Eastside's association with productive labour gave way to another long-standing association: "morally dubious" activities such as gambling, alcohol consumption and prostitution (Robertson and Culhane 2005; Sommers and Blomley 2005; Hasson and Ley 1994). For generations, the area had been called "skid road," named for the streets that were marked by long corduroy grooves designed to slide logs in to the water. As the neighbourhood became increasingly identified as a space of contamination, moral transgression and decline, its transition from "skid road" to "skid row" gradually took hold. Yet by the 1970s, activists and area residents had begun to challenge this title and its attendant stigmatization. The name "Downtown Eastside" was born of these struggles, as advocates sought to erase the neighbourhood's typecasting and "create new ways of imagining and representing the place" (Sommers 1998: 287–88). Yet, while renaming has restored a certain dignity to the area and served as a potent symbol of its residents' political vitality, much of this original stigmatization persists, albeit in different forms.

Press accounts that today map the Downtown Eastside as a space of generalized chaos reproduce the impression of a city spatially divided between order and disorder. This presumed separation is rendered natural by patterns of omission and minimization that obscure vital historical and material connections between city spaces. As Sommers and Blomley (2002: 53) put it, "zones of darkness and despair and the zone of happy prosperity are parts of the same city." But if we refuse to accept that spatial concentrations of poverty and prosperity are simply the product of a neutral and organic process of development, then we must ask what forces have contributed to the production of these stark divisions (Razack 2002). We can begin to historicize and unmap this imagined separation by demonstrating some of the core connections between the spaces of supposed chaos and order. Razack's (2002: 5) contention that "unmapping" naturalized geographies requires not only "asking how spaces came to be" but also interrogating the "world views that rest upon [them]," is particularly relevant here. Building on this dual objective, the discussion that follows will demonstrate how patterns of capital disinvestment and reinvestment, private and institutional strategies of containment and political violence have hastened and produced the stark socio-economic cleavages that exist between the spaces of urban Vancouver but also ask how particular ideological assumptions operate to naturalize these divisions.

The presumption that the Downtown Eastside has been "taken over" by a criminal underclass that has both created and hastened the area's deterioration jars against the patterns of economic restructuring and capital disinvestment that facilitated its transition from a bustling hub of urban commerce to its (assumed) contemporary status as a zone of degeneracy. At the end of the Second World War, the commercial core of what is now the Downtown Eastside was a thriving agglomeration of retail shops, places of employment, entertainment venues and bustling city streets. On any given day, thousands would arrive in the district by foot, ferry, or one of the many Interurban streetcars that stationed at the southwest corner of Hastings and Carrall streets; they would cycle in and out of a rich urban fabric accented by celebrated theatres (the Bijou, the Electric, the Lux), elegant hotels (the Woods, for example, which was the first to offer private telephone service in each of its ninety rooms) and the best window shopping west of Winnipeg. The commercial king of the bustling Downtown Eastside was George Woodward's landmark department store, which lorded above its rivals from a seven-storey throne at the corner of Hastings and Abott streets (Mackie 2008). It was here — amongst smartly dressed elevator attendants and glistening shop-floor display cases — that the much commemorated "10-cent Days" promotion rose to regional fame, with incremental price increases throughout the decades (Hudson's Bay Company 2009). Of course, the area was not merely a hub of conventionally enriching entertainment and wholesome consumptive behaviour. The Carall Street docks were also the point of entry for thousands of resource workers returning from seasonal gigs at remote cannery and logging operations in the province's interior (Hasson and Ley 1994). The composition of the Downtown Eastside's built environment reflected the diverse needs of this cohort and a wide range of brothels, burlesque houses and beer parlours were there to ensure that they were satisfied.

By the early 1960s, however, sweeping economic changes began to sap the neighbourhood of its vitality. Remote industrial employers were relying less on seasonal workers and the large transient workforce that had once spent off-seasons in the neighbourhood gradually began to dwindle (Francis 2006). Mills and manufacturers once centred in the urban core began to move out of the city as their owners sought cheaper land and proximity to roadways. At the same time, retail merchants faced the impacts of suburbanization, which had begun to push shopping districts to the urban periphery. Limited parking and streets not intended for use by cars made the Downtown peninsula hazardous for drivers. The built landscape and its stock of commercially zoned buildings, meanwhile, were increasingly considered "unsuited to the needs of a modern downtown" (Sommers and Blomley 2002: 34). Yet the decisive blow to the Downtown Eastside's prosperity came with changes to transportation patterns. In the late 1950s, ferry service from North Vancouver was terminated just as a major steamship corporation — which, for decades, had unloaded passengers in the area — ceased its operations. Almost simultaneously, interurban streetcar service was abandoned along with its Carrall Street terminal (Mackie 2008). For decades, these services had delivered thousands of people to the district every day. Suddenly, that source of vitality was gone.

In the years that followed, the Downtown Eastside slipped into a pattern of sharp decline. Real-estate values in the neighbourhood began to sag, facilitating a wide availability of affordable housing and attracting increasing numbers of low-income people. Its sprawling network of single-room-occupancy hotels (SROs) — which accounted for more than 13,000 units of housing in the 1970s — had once provided homes for many on fixed incomes, particularly single men who had worked in the province's resource industries (Condon 2007; Blomley 2004). From the 1960s on, industrial and manufacturing jobs declined in British Columbia as official priorities shifted towards promoting service-industry sectors of the economy. In Vancouver, this transition was so pronounced that by the mid-1980s some were already referring to the city as "post-industrial" (Punter 2003). In this context, the population of resource workers still living in the neighbourhood began to dwindle; those who remained were something of a historical residue, the last living vestiges of a bygone era. By the 1980s, new generations of low-income people had begun to move in and replace them. The Downtown Eastside remained one of the few city spaces where affordable housing could still be secured while housing prices had soared all around it. Yet, by the late 1980s, things had begun to change. The pressures of an "overheated" property market coupled with the abundance of cheap Downtown Eastside land zoned for high densities began to attract a new wave of capital reinvestment in the area (Blomley 2004).

The return of capital did not result in wholesale gentrification; urban transformations have developed in spotty, uneven patterns. Certain pockets of the neighbourhood were aggressively redeveloped and dramatically improved while others languished or further declined. The district now known as Gastown, for example, was the target of considerable regeneration efforts in the 1980s and 1990s and now bears little resemblance to the urban decay to its immediate east. There is now a striking statistical divergence between Gastown and its surrounding areas (Smith 2003).

Planners had originally conceived the development to be a "site of inclusiveness" and contrasted their practices with established corporate and bureaucratic development strategies (Smith 2003: 501). Gastown's designation as a heritage zone promised a different kind of development, one that planners hoped would simultaneously preserve some of the city's original building stock and be a catalyst to a broader revitalization. But heritage status required private property owners that were willing to bankroll the considerable costs of upgrades and preservations. Rental and condominium prices began to reflect this necessity (Smith 2003). As Sommers and Blomley (2002: 41) observe, the heritage preservation scheme was, in the end, little more than an "economic and property development strategy." As Gastown developed as a bastion of prosperity and conspicuous consumption — developments that heritage designation had directly afforded — the "undesignated" spaces of nearby Hastings Street sunk into a pattern of accelerated decline accented by structural deterioration, increased drug activity and widespread commercial vacancy (Smith 2003). Tourism Vancouver's (2008) sanguine suggestion that visitors "be mindful that Gastown, while very safe, is partially located in a more graphic part of the city" understates the stark divisions that are laid bare at the area's borders. The decline of Hastings Street has facilitated an explosion of storefront vacancies. Between Cambie and Main Streets, commercial vacancies had been as low as 13 percent in 1986 but shot up to 36 percent by 1996; by 2001 the street's notorious 100 block had a vacancy rate of 50 percent, a level that would grow to 57 percent by 2007 (City of Vancouver 2006).

The Gastown/Hastings comparison offers an illustrative example of the growing polarization that has come to typify the neighbourhood. As redeveloped districts have become increasingly occupied by a wealthy elite, a correlative scarcity of affordable housing has worked to concentrate low-income people in particular areas. Put differently, simultaneous patterns of investment and disinvestment that have defined area development since the 1980s have facilitated a process that has seen the neighbourhood increasingly divided by class. Importantly, these spaces of concentrated poverty have increasingly become the residuum of populations adversely affected by a host of structural forces. In certain ways, they act as "collection zones" for people dispossessed by the ongoing effects of colonialism, marginalized by retrenchments of the welfare state, released to the street by the widespread deinstitutionalizations of mental health facilities and stricken by the exigencies of addiction (Lowman 2000). Too often, however, these broader structural factors have been subsumed by narrations that label these spaces of the marginalized as spaces of self-selected degeneracy and a vile criminality.

Patterns of capital investment and disinvestment are not themselves sufficient to explain how the Downtown Eastside has come to be stigmatized as a zone of urban chaos. As I argue previously, the presence of the low-track sex trade and of open drug markets have been central to the development of this reputation. Yet dominant accounts which suggest that the presence of these industries have acted as a magnet attracting criminality towards them occlude the well-established history of geographical eviction and enforcement that has operated to concentrate these practices in the Downtown Eastside.

Historical accounts of prostitution in Vancouver have demonstrated that police and civic authorities have long tolerated prostitution in some city spaces while aggressively purging it from others. Deborah Nilsen's (1980) study of the city's pre-war industry, for example, demonstrates a long-standing tolerance so long as commercial sex remained confined to the more proletarian districts of the city's East. Lowman's (1986, 1992b, 2000) studies of prostitution in Vancouver from the 1970s to the present reveal a similar pattern of geographically specific tolerance. He demonstrates that outdoor strolls have operated with little interruption for generations on Vancouver's Eastside while various "outbreaks" of prostitution in the city's more well-heeled areas have been met with aggressive deployments of coercive state power. For example, Lowman points to the 1976 closure of two downtown cabaret clubs as one decisive moment when prostitution was constituted as a "social problem" that merited intervention. The closures pushed indoor workers to the outdoor strolls and many began to operate in the West end. Media narratives both generated and consolidated popular outrage as business owners and area residents began to demand that officials launch a "clean-up." They contended that their streets had been overtaken by a prostitution boom. Yet, as Lowman points out, the industry had actually changed very little as a result of the closures. What had altered fundamentally was its visibility. Nevertheless, the perception of a prostitution "explosion" gave rise to the formation of a series of local residents' groups dedicated to securing the industry's eviction from certain spaces. Throughout the late 1970s and 1980s, groups that were "conspicuously absent when street prostitution had been confined to the less salubrious areas of the downtown core" did battle with sex workers (Lowman 1986: 13).

The most effective of these was the Concerned Residents of the West End (CROWE) who demanded that their area be purged of prostitution "no matter where it might end up" (Lowman 1992b: 7). Over the course of several years, the group managed to win a series of significant concessions, including the installation of traffic diverting barriers, a short-lived civic by-law and eventually a rare civil nuisance injunction issued by the provincial state. Yet, as Lowman notes, what was particularly exceptional about the injunction was its geographic specificity. The order applied only to workers operating in a small, and particularly wealthy, group of West End city blocks (Lowman 1992b). And while, ultimately, the measures were largely successful in evicting prostitutes from the area, their primary effect was to simply displace the industry to other areas. Accordingly, new resident groups and business associations came together to challenge prostitution as it began to operate in other city spaces. Yet none were quite as successful as CROWE in eliciting the coercion of the state.

Activists in less-affluent Mount Pleasant, where many evicted from the West End had ended up, demanded to know why the province would not enact a similar injunction on their behalf. Only after considerable effort, including a direct-action "shame the johns" campaign, were they successful in securing police cooperation in evicting the industry. Here again, evictions simply displaced the industry and most workers began operating in the Strathcona neighbourhood of the Downtown Eastside where sex workers received a decidedly less hostile response. As Lowman (1992b: 11–12) notes, "residents of Strathcona must have wondered why a similar police effort was not made to deal with problems in their neighbourhood" but "generally a very different approach was taken ... in responding to street prostitution in this, the poorest area of Vancouver."

While these particular developments coincide with a period of uncertainty about the legal enforcement of prostitution and thus cannot be considered independently of broader debates, they nevertheless seem to demonstrate a direct correlation between the economic power of complainants and the coercive effort of the state. Residents in the West End managed to secure rare and provocative state action while residents in Mount Pleasant struggled for a far less significant deployment of force. Meanwhile, enforcement in the Downtown Eastside/Strathcona remained minimal. In fact, as Lowman has argued, police intervention in Eastside street prostitution has had a tendency to peak only at moments when police have been interested in cracking down on narcotics distribution and have found it useful to "identify female addicts and create a pool of potential informers in the process of discovering heroin traffickers" (Lowman 1986: 13). In much the same way, open drug markets — such as the one at the intersection of Main and Hastings — have been met with a degree of tolerance that would be almost unimaginable in more affluent zones. Among the ruins of this disinvested and decaying landscape, illicit activity has received far less coercive attention than it has elsewhere.

Though seemingly disconnected, patterns of disinvestment in the Downtown Eastside and patterns of geographically specific tolerance of illicit activity offer potent ways to interrogate the hollowness of the claim that Vancouver's inner city has been "taken over" by a degenerate population. Taken together, these historical patterns not only demonstrate how the presumed "chaos" of the Downtown Eastside has been produced and sustained by political and structural forces, but they also lay bare an acute relationship between power and space. This relationship hinges on certain ideological assumptions and, in particular, notions of ownership and entitlement. Blomley (2003) contends that in liberal societies many have become accustomed to considering law and violence as antithetical. People in liberal societies have tended to imagine violence as something "outside of the law" and as "that which contains and prevents an anomic anarchy" (Blomely 2003: 121). Yet notions of private possession of territory are intimately woven into this world view and its legal codes; the assumed entitlements that ownership produces have frequently realized particular forms of violence. Thus, as Blomley (2003: 129) puts it, "at its core property entails the legitimate act of expulsion, devolved to the state."

The series of Vancouver stroll evictions that I describe above offer striking examples of a view of rights that valorizes private ownership. Each of the residents' groups that sought to purge the industry from their streets were animated by the shared assumption that a private citizen should expect authorities to ensure its "civil right … to be protected from the nuisance said to be caused by street prostitution" (Lowman 1992a: 85). While previous anti-prostitution campaigns had focused on notions of moral contamination, "social hygiene" and even "white slavery," these modern efforts were driven by an assumed entitlement to "peace" in private residential spaces. Lowman (1992a: 86) describes the logic of CROWE's demands for eviction:

> it was argued that prostitutes offended citizens by harassing them on the street and that the residents' right to peace and quiet was violated by the noise made by prostitutes, customers, and onlookers late at night. Customers, by indiscriminately requesting services, offended non-

prostitutes traveling through the strolls. Taken together, these nuisances were alleged to reduce property values and increase crime in a mutually reinforcing relationship that would ultimately destroy the residential communities in which the strolls were located.

Notions of order and chaos are central here. The liberal view of rights and the centrality of its valorization of private ownership operate to legitimate and naturalize the expectation of order in private spaces.

Henri Lefevbre's (1991) celebrated notion of a bureaucratized and commodified "abstract space" is particularly instructive here. Such enclosures demand "a concerted attempt to define the appropriate meaning of, and suitable activities that can take place within" the boundaries of a privatized space (McCann 2002: 69). As Lefebvre describes it:

> [abstract space]… is a space… of growing homogeneity… a police space in which the state tolerates no resistance and no obstacles. [It] implies tacit agreement, a non-aggression pact, a contract, as it were, of non-violence… In the street, each individual is supposed not to attack those he meets; anyone who transgresses this law is deemed guilty of a criminal act… This economy valorizes certain relationships between people in particular places and thus gives rise to connotive discourses concerning these places; these in turn, generate "consensuses" or conventions according to which, for example, such and such a place is supposed to be trouble-free, a quiet area where people go peacefully to have a good time, and so forth. (quoted in McCann 2002: 69)

Interestingly, spaces of capital disinvestment — which in Vancouver tend to be spaces of racialized poverty — seem to be spaces where a certain "chaos" is permitted by the state. They are zones that are, in some sense, deemed outside of the public purview. As Razack (2002: 9) points out, the representation of "public" space as a "unity which must be protected from conflict," presents a "compelling example of how we might consider space as a social product by attending to [the] social hierarchies" that such representations reveal. Enforcement practices reaffirm this hierarchical imaginary. For example, barriers, civic by-laws and nuisance injunctions designed to curb prostitution produce sex workers as illegitimate occupiers of space while its opponents — those who are supposedly "peaceful" — are produced as the "legitimate users and natural owners of the public space" (Razack 2002: 10). This assumed entitlement justifies the violence of eviction.

Yet, as Blomley has argued, the hegemony of a liberal view of rights in which the "ownership model" is central is not merely static and stable. By contrast, it requires a sustained enactment and reproduction in order to ensure its perpetuation. The persuasiveness of this model is in part due to its realization in actual space; the sustained effectiveness of such persuasion demands "a continual active doing"

(Blomley 2004: 122). Taking this cue, we might consider how narrations of chaos (which, as I will demonstrate, are abundant in the coverage) are key ideological vehicles through which the enactment and valorization of private property is accomplished. The "chaos" of the Downtown Eastside is not itself distinct from the supposed order of other spaces. By contrast, the forces that have sustained the latter have also concentrated the former. Through a persistent contrasting of the "peace" of neighbourhoods where responsible private ownership prevails and the "chaos" of spaces where private capital has largely fled (not withstanding the few "fleabag" hotel owners, of course), the coverage tacitly valorizes and enacts the legitimacy of private spaces.

The ideological dissection of urban Vancouver between these apparently distinct spaces produces a "frontier" which both symbolically and materially delineates a sharp spatial divide between "contending constituencies." Neil Smith's (1996) work on the transformation of Manhattan's Lower East Side in the late 1980s demonstrates how the language of "frontier" was employed to justify capital's conquest of the neighbourhood. He argues that a "gentrification frontier" came to denote the fundamental divide between the civil spaces of ordered capital and the disordered chaos presumed to be festering on the other side of its material and moral line. He demonstrates how gentrification efforts produced a new manifestation of the courageous "pioneer" charged with the task of penetrating the dark spaces of disordered chaos and establishing the first bulwarks of civility. As Blomley (2004: 179) has observed, Smith's formulation has demonstrated the relevance of the "frontier" image to the "moral and political terrain of gentrification." In fact, the discursive formulation of the spaces on the outside of the gentrification frontier as an "urban wilderness [of] savagery and chaos, awaiting the urban homesteaders who can forge a renaissance of hope and civility" strike a haunting note of harmony with the description of the Downtown Eastside privileged by the coverage studied (Blomley 2004: 179). If we consider the neighbourhood, as reporter Rosie DiManno would have us do, as a space "where hope fades to black," then the new urban "pioneer" — those brave souls willing to purchase property in the neighbourhood — is produced less as an "invader" who will hasten the eviction of the poor and more as a courageous citizen who will begin to restore some order to the zone of chaos.

Developers have already begun to seek out this new generation of "pioneers." In 1999, for example, developer John Stovell explained to the Toronto Star that successfully marketing the area would require attracting an adventuring new demographic (Eurchuk 2007). He remarked:

> We can't sanitize the area or convince people it's pristine. We're looking for a more youthful, risk-oblivious person… As soon as it's seen as the cool place to be they'll be crawling over the bodies to get there. (quoted in Eurchuk 2007)

Meanwhile, Vancouver's "king" of the condo market, Bob Rennie, has targeted the neighbourhood's "character" as its primary selling point, encouraging brave pioneers to capitalize on culture rather than settle for sterile suburban comfort (Eurchuk 2007). As he puts it:

> [the Downtown Eastside] is an authentic area, not a sanitized environment. Neighbourhoods like this are rare and offer a creative mix of cutting-edge culture, heritage and character. This in the home of the future ... be bold or move to suburbia. (quoted in Eurchuk 2007)

Rennie's pitch is reminiscent of Smith's description of a new generation of artists and "creative professionals" who operated as the initial shock troops in the conquest of Manhattan's Lower Eastside. Smith (1996: 27) argues that "squalor, poverty, and the violence of eviction [were] constituted as exquisite ambience" for this first wave of gentrifiers. He notes how "rapid polarization" becomes "glorified for its excitement rather than condemned for its violence or understood for the rage it threatens" (Smith 1996: 27).

Connections between the gentrification frontier and the historical frontier of colonial expansion have a particular significance in Vancouver (Blomley 2004). Just as the occupied territories of British Columbia appeared as an empty territory ripe for settlement to colonial conquerors, so the Downtown Eastside has appeared as a "terra nullius to some developers." Blomley (2004: 92) writes:

> The similarities with the ideologies that undergirded the colonial dispossession of native peoples are striking. Deemed mobile, native peoples could not be seen as enjoying any legitimate entitlement given the supposed conjunction of permanence and possession.

There are, of course, dramatic distinctions between the scales of violence that occurred at the historical frontier and the contemporary frontiers of gentrification and we should be very weary about conflating the two. Nevertheless, both offer potent ways to consider how symbolic constructions, particularly constructions of an absence, can be employed to justify catastrophic violence.

Mapping Chaos

The dominant narratives that emerge from the coverage are strikingly geographic. They both situate the crisis of Vancouver's missing and murdered women in actual space and provide compelling ways to understand that space. Their explanations of the crisis are inseparable from a particular branding of the "mean streets" of the Downtown Eastside which functions as a constitutive backdrop to the coverage; it marks the core symbolic terrain on which the crisis itself is mapped.

The metaphor of the map is instructive here; cartographic practices of signification share striking commonalities with the processes of "territorial socialization" that I describe in this chapter. Just as maps allow cartographers to impose an abstract coherence on the illimitable multiplicity of the physical landscape, so too do homogenizing representations of the Downtown Eastside impose a reductive narrative coherence on the heterogeneity of the neighbourhood's social and political topography. Below, I demonstrate how the coverage examined operates to actively map the neighbourhood as a space of chaos. First, I argue that a journalistic fixation on neighbourhood spaces where disorder is most apparent reproduces a deceptively narrow view of the area. Next, I consider how two distinct but complimentary discourses contribute to and consolidate an impression of generalized chaos. The first produces the neighbourhood as a space of general foulness — as an area consumed by a pervasive filth that contaminates both the bodies of residents and the built landscape that envelopes them. The second produces the neighbourhood as enclosure consumed by criminality and physical endangerment. Lastly, I return to the ideological implications of this branding. I argue that it naturalizes marginality and reifies the imagined distance between city spaces that I have begun to explain above (Walkowitz 1992).

Chaos as Press Narrative

Press narratives generated by the investigation and prosecution of Robert Pickton yield a powerful mix of visual and textual cues that reinforce the distinct impression of a neighbourhood consumed by degeneracy and disorder. The appellation "skid row" re-appears frequently, a discursive move that not only harkens back to the neighbourhood's previous characterization, but also taps into the well-established chain of associations that this term has come to denote in the broader culture.

Dozens of references to the neighbourhood appear in the coverage. Most are peripheral mentions in narratives concerned with case developments. Nevertheless, many of these casual references are instrumental in reinforcing the themes of the skid-row categorization. The words "Downtown Eastside" are routinely coupled with pejorative adjectives — the neighbourhood is described variously as "seamy," "seedy," "squalid," "lurid," "wretched," as a "scar of a place" and even "terrible," to note just a few examples. Yet, while these depictions are important, the series of articles that take the neighbourhood itself as their subject and attempt a more comprehensive consideration of it accomplish the most substantial reinforcements of this stigmatization. Six articles in the coverage offer such direct reflections and attempt to contextualize the broader case by providing thorough accounts of the spaces where the missing and murdered women lived and worked. There is little variation between these definitional accounts. Each provides a startling portrait of open narcotic transaction and consumption, deranged and dazed individuals and a decayed and dirtied urban landscape. Most are first-person accounts of a "daring" journalistic foray into the dark urban recesses. They create the distinct impression that few from mainstream society would dare to meander into these spaces intentionally. It is imagined as a "mean enclave" with little to offer people from the straight world, its dark recesses are said to invite only particular kinds of "newcomer[s]," those "lost souls... lured by the promise of easy drugs" (Mason 2007). DiManno (2007a) tells her readers that "nobody comes here just to watch, as in famous tenderloin districts elsewhere." Evidently, her assertion excludes the throng of journalists "drawn as moths to flames to document, analyze [and] represent... the dramatic and photogenic spectacle of social suffering in this neighbourhood" (Culhane 2003: 594).

The Downtown Eastside spans a network of twenty-one city blocks but press interest in the area is largely restricted to the spaces where social disorder and criminality are plainly visible. Of the six texts which focus on the neighbourhood, five refer directly to chaotic scenes unfolding on notorious Hastings Street, while the other's allusions to "open drug markets" and vivid imagery of "junkies shooting up in alleyways... prostitutes openly having sex behind buildings... drunks puking on sidewalks" largely accomplish the same effect (Mason 2007). These articles reveal a pronounced journalistic preference to produce the neighbourhood in a particular way. In their efforts to locate the grim epicentre of the crisis — the spaces where Pickton is said to have preyed — reporters have unfolded a pattern of representation that over-privileges certain aspects of the area while erasing others entirely. The result is the impression of an area consumed by "chaos."

This characterization is illustrated by the three articles that describe events at the corner of Main and Hastings streets. The intersection, often described as the area's central hub of illicit activity, is a perennial target for journalists interested in lurid displays of public criminality, including those covering the trial of Robert Pickton. In one *Toronto Star* article, Girard (2002b) describes the area as a wasteland of illicit activity where degeneracy swirls at a "dizzying pace." His observations are accented by a provocative photograph of a woman using a car mirror to inject heroin into her neck. Describing the intersection, he writes:

> A parade of men and women thrust crumpled bills at a man doling out vials of crack cocaine.
>
> Some go down alleyways or into nearby public washrooms to smoke it, while others flick on their lighters and inhale, oblivious to the traffic whizzing by.
>
> One transvestite in a pink miniskirt holds court while a barefoot woman wearing a once-elegant purple dress wanders down the sidewalk. A man with two bicycles, one for him, the other for his partner selling crack at $10 a gram, chews on a used syringe and talks to himself while dancing to a song playing in his head. (Girard 2002b)

In a similar *Globe and Mail* story, published the previous day, reporter Alexandra Gill (2002) describes the same corner. Her report is accented by a large photograph of a woman smoking crack in a filth-strewn alleyway and a line-up of closely cropped images of the missing and murdered women which connects her portrait to the broader case. In the left corner, a map labeled the "seedy side of town" situates her story relative to other city spaces. She writes:

> At the corner of Main and Hastings Streets, many of the addicts, pushers and prostitutes swarming on the streets yesterday at noon hadn't heard about the breakthrough in the case of the 50 women who have disappeared from the neighbourhood.
>
> At the down-an-out epicentre of Vancouver's seamy Downtown Eastside, most had more urgent matters to attend to. Like the woman down on her knees trying to inject heroin into her friend's neck as people walked by.
>
> The second woman, sprawled on her back, certainly wasn't in any mood to chat. "Ahh," she screamed, bolting upright as her partner missed her jugular vein, again. (Gill 2002)

Similarly, in a front page story that ran in the first week of the trial, the *Toronto Star's* Rosie DiManno (2007a) returns to this very corner:

> At the corner of Hastings and Main, an open market for heroin and cocaine, a man punches a woman in the mouth. She shrieks and lunges at his face, nails clawing. Few among the dozens milling outside the Carnegie Community Centre take notice of the episode.
>
> Around the corner, in a laneway where a health clinic hands out clean syringes and condoms, sickly teenage girls are smoking crack behind a skip, the brief buzz just numbing enough to send them back out for the next ten-dollar-trick.
>
> It all happens brazenly, kitty corner from a police station, patrol cars moving slowly through the phalanx of bodies, narrowed eyes looking into vacant eyes.

These representations are significant not merely as an index of recurring place. They also demonstrate, through an exclusive privileging of those neighbourhood spaces where "criminality" is plainly observed, the coverage's more general univocality. Eclipsed by these narrations (which are themselves paradigmatic of the pattern of spatial descriptions which suffuse the coverage) are the 16,000 residents who have little connection to illicit activity. As Culhane (2003: 594) notes, many are simply "too poor to live anywhere else in Canada's highest rent city." Yet this population is consigned to the margins; they are rendered invisible by a culture of journalism more interested in the dramatic spectacle of criminal transaction than interrogating less visible forms of social and economic dislocation. The neighbourhood's well-established history of vibrant interpersonal solidarity, political mobilization and grassroots activism is silenced by images that imply a generalized break of social cohesion. The part comes to represent the whole as the repeated and nearly exclusive invocation of deviant spaces operates to stigmatize the entire neighbourhood.

The coverage also produces the Downtown Eastside as a place of ubiquitous filth. The quotations above offer a few indications of this characterization but are merely parts of what amounts to a widespread representational pattern. Themes of impurity saturate the coverage as a whole. Imagery of a built landscape in a state of terminal decline fuse almost seamlessly with images of diseased and dirty individuals. They connect with a well-established tradition of representing the neighbourhood as a space of filth and contagion.

Sommers and Blomley (2002: 22-25) point to particular panics over narcotics and HIV as central to this construction. They contend that these and other decisive events have been at the core of a "rhetoric of pathology" which has fused the "body of the urban outcast" with the "body of the city" in three central ways. First, the neighbourhood itself was defined as an "insidious zone" of contaminated spaces, which has engendered and reproduced its own set of problems. Second, the "poor and drug addicted" were defined as agents of contamination directly responsible for urban decay and widespread disinvestment. Third, residents themselves were imagined as "morally isolated from the rest of the city" as the assumed interconnection of destitution, addiction and disease operated to situate the neighbourhood "as a place radically different from anywhere else in Vancouver" (Sommers and Blomley 2002: 22–25).

These patterns are reproduced in the coverage in a number of ways. Particular signifiers of filth and contagion recur with marked frequency. Images of crack pipes, used syringes and fast food packaging, to name a few, appear repeatedly in descriptions of the neighbourhood. These images imply that neighbourhood filth is produced by filthy occupants, and individual disregard for neighbourhood spaces is constructed as the core causal condition of their foulness. Gill's (2002) investigation of the neighbourhood's "down-and-out epicentre" offers a potent example of how this impression is produced. Her interview with "George," a neighbourhood resident, demonstrates the connection between human practices and omnipresent filth. She writes:

> "There's nothing to talk about" he said, spitting a fat glob of phlegm on to a sidewalk already awash in needle wrappers, ketchup packages and cigarette butts. (Gill 2002)

Undoubtedly chosen for their capacity to repulse, such images are common to a series of narrative accounts that mark residents not only as consistent with the decay that surrounds them but also as its partial authors. Descriptions of filthy streets frequently appear alongside images of area residents intimately integrated with their polluted surroundings. Photographs of women using drugs fuse with textual descriptions that find people "sprawled out" on their backs, hunched over on industrial loading bays, and "squatted" dazed on a sidewalk, usually as they smoke crack or inject heroin. Those who live in the neighbourhood are produced as creatures of its corners rather than residents of its housing stock.

This "creature" motif connects to representations of decay in the built landscape. Accounts that privilege the contamination of physical spaces — Girard's (2002b) impression of a "grim collection of filthy alleyways, derelict buildings and shattered dreams," for example — mirror descriptions which privilege contaminated physical bodies. There is a representational harmony between the characterization of individuals as the wanton producers of filth and infection and the characterization of a built landscape that has been treated with an analogous disregard. So imagined, physical deterioration can be explained by the very presence of a "foul" underclass and not, for example, housing regulation schemes that encourage landlords to leave residential hotels in disrepair or the particular exigencies of a market logic that has facilitated widespread capital disinvestment in the area.

Urban Disconnections

Perhaps most centrally, however, the conflation of images of foul bodies and images of a foul landscape reproduce the impression of a neighbourhood radically dislocated from other city spaces. Images of the dilapidated network of residential hotels or "garbage strewn" alleyways are contrasted against the "treelined streets and open spaces" of other Vancouver neighbourhoods. Girard (2002b), for example, demonstrates palpable shock that "all this" (referring to a lurid scene he's just described) can unfold just "a short walk" from places where "tourists wander" beneath "the spectacular snow capped mountains of Vancouver's north shore tower a few kilometers — and a world — away." Such images reinforce and directly identify a "monumental divide." A constant invocation of the urban alleyway, for example, taps into a series of well-established nefarious associations. In popular culture, such spaces have long been employed as zones of danger. Removed from the relative safety of the main thoroughfare, the alleyway has not only come to signify a space of illicit transaction and dubious dealing, but also the scavenging ground of vagrant and vermin alike. News narratives that situate street-involved people in these spaces — accounts, for example, which locate residents "shooting up in alleyways" or loitering around the "back-alley" entrances that are usually "staked out by hookers" — inevitably evoke these well established meanings.

Constant references to physical violence also produce the Downtown Eastside as a space of danger. The neighbourhood is produced as a space of constant physical aggression, a horrifying Hobbesian enclosure where the war of *all against all* is waged with unyielding fury. Such accounts establish interpersonal solidarity and cooperation as aberrant and brutality as the norm. Reports from the neighbourhood draw on first person accounts that describe beatings, stabbings, unprovoked attacks, physical disputes over drugs or territory and crazed predation as part of a daily pattern of violence in the area. Street-involved people, including sex workers, are described as at the constant mercy of predatory landlords, "poverty pimps," violent customers and dealers. One reporter sums this view up bluntly: "there is, in fact, no refuge" (DiManno 2007a). Another *National Post* report (Hutchinson 2007) draws on an interview with a former sex worker to illustrate this impression of constant terror:

> The people who work here know they may be attacked at any time, says Ms. Allan.
> They are always on edge, 24 hours a day. They are in fight or flight mode. The next guy to come along might just want her company. Or he could be [convicted rapist and serial killer] Ted Bundy.

And shortly below, it continues:

> We pause beside a bridge about a block from Ms. Allan's former "spot" where she used to stand and wait for customers. A woman she knew was brazenly beaten here three years ago, left for dead atop some busy railroad tracks; it wasn't the first incident of its kind.

Yet reports suggest that it is not merely the grim figures of underworld authority — pimps, dangerous customers and extortionist landlords — who denizens of the neighbourhood must be wary of. Street-involved people, they contend, must also be cautious of each other in this space where self-preservation is the only law and no other can be trusted. As one statement attributed to a street-involved woman puts it, "nobody cares for anybody but themselves" (Girard 2002b).

This vision of an unyielding interpersonal struggle is consolidated by images that suggest a general desensitization to violence in the neighbourhood. In one of the accounts quoted above, for example, a man brazenly punches a woman in the mouth while few among the dozens congregated "take notice of the episode" (DiManno 2007a). Moreover, the above descriptions of congregated people at the corner of Main and Hastings (and many similar portrayals) create the impression of a population too consumed by addictions to take basic personal precautions. Girard's descriptions of people so oblivious that they chew on used syringes or walk barefoot among a sea of discarded ones gives the impression of a population that is indeed "too strung out to care." Interpersonal cooperation, such descriptions suggest, is constantly thwarted by the fiendish imperatives of the addicted. They create the impression of a radical divide between the self-interested space of the addict, where assault and abuse occur "brazenly" and without notice, and the ordered spaces where such transgressions would be met with significant consequence. The space of the addicted is presented as a space where human civility is subordinated to animal desire, an impression consolidated by the frequent deployment of animalian language. Take, for example, the descriptions of the intersection at Main and Hastings cited above. Here alone, we find "pushers and prostitutes" who "swarm" together, a woman who "shrieks and lunges" with "nails clawing," and men and women who "thrust" crumpled bills with a fiendish urgency. Such descriptions have a distancing effect; they demonstrate the radical alterity of an inner city space where all sense of a common "peace" seems to have broken down.

Reporters repeatedly suggest that the Downtown Eastside functions as a "magnet" drawing ever greater numbers into its dark orbit, in spite of its assumed status as a space of danger and degeneracy. Mason (2007) observes in the *Globe and Mail*:

> [the neighbourhood] has become a delirious lure for the drug-addled … It would be easier to get drugs there, they figured, than on the streets of Campbell River or Vernon or Cache Creek. So they fled their communities to assume mostly tragic existences in the Downtown Eastside, existences that quickly included dirty needles and dirty tricks, rat-infested hotel rooms and often an early death.

Access to illicit markets is marked as a primary force driving new waves of migration to the neighbourhood. New recruits are thought to favour residence here for its proximity to narcotics and the sex industry. As such, the neighbourhood becomes mapped not only as a space of degeneracy, but as a place of self-selected degeneracy.

So conceived, political intervention aimed at alleviating some of the area's problems takes on an air of futility. Thus, for Mason (2007): "despite the best intentions of police and politicians over the years" the area "remains as miserable and depressing a place as there is in North America." Or, for Girard (2002b): "governments at all levels have developed various programs aimed at improving life for area residents… but… at the epicentre of the downtown eastside … it appears … that those attempts have met with little success." The state can do little, according to this logic, for people that are more interested in feeding their addictions than participating in any restorative or ameliorative social schemes. While undoubtedly proactive government efforts have achieved important gains in the neighbourhood and the power of addiction to some degree has drawn people to the neighbourhood, these observations overstate the reach of both.

The prevailing pessimism that such descriptions engender connects with the broader contention that the neighbourhood has become a drain on the public purse and that the "public" has seen little result for their investment. As DiManno (2007c) puts it "millions of dollars have been poured into the poverty sinkhole that is the Downtown Eastside ... with no one quite knowing where that money is going." Meanwhile, she observes, "poverty pimps" and even "poverty empires" have "taken root." And while she does go on to acknowledge that a lack of detoxification facilities has exacerbated problems, her initial observations bolster a more pessimistic view of the prospects for change. Analyses that define the neighbourhood as a space where a self-selected group of deviants willingly congregate have the effect of rendering that group responsible for the danger and decline that they are said to be immersed in. Crucially, such narrations offer a limited and dehistoricized impression of the forces that have contributed to the neighbourhood's concentration of illicit activity, poverty and physical decline. They mask the contradictions in public policy and private development that have, in effect, actively contributed to the material production of this space. As such, they offer an important ideological rationale for "cleaning up" the neighbourhood. Indeed, coercive intervention, in this view, might be conceived as a necessary step in the restoration of the order that has been uprooted by this illegitimate occupation of city spaces.

The despised practices of public deviance mark the occupants of the Downtown Eastside as fundamentally other. As Sommers and Blomley (2002) observe, the reproduction of images which suggest a space devoid of productive ends and productive people lends itself to the view that this urban space, a core part of Vancouver's "historical entitlement," has been left to ruin by a disinterested "urban underclass" that has hastened its seepage into a bog of terminal decline. They argue that the landscapes of decay scattered along Hastings Street invite outsiders to conclude that "it is no longer 'our' neighbourhood." So conceived, the only way that the "valued landscape" of the area can be saved is "with the removal of that which threatens it — the poor — and its replacement by citizens who are better equipped to reclaim its potential" (Sommers and Blomley 2002: 49).

Such characterizations have several important consequences. In the first place, they obscure the symbiotic material interconnection of seemingly distinct city spaces. Secondly, they valorize particular kinds of urban occupancy through a negative representation of their presumed opposite. In this view, what the Downtown Eastside lacks is positive kinds of occupancy, neighbourhood dwellers who are invested in its renewal. Indeed, there is something of this view in Mason's (2007) assessment of the neighbourhood's "problems." He writes:

> The Downtown Eastside is unhealthy not just because there are drugs, prostitution and homelessness concentrated. It's unhealthy because so many problems are concentrated there. Every unhealthy person who goes there sees only someone like himself. There is no "normal" to which to aspire.

In this view, what the "low-other" of the Downtown Eastside lacks is a role model, an exemplar of middle class social norms and appropriate neighbourhood stewardship.

More generally, however, we might consider how the space of the Downtown Eastside, and the impressions of particular kinds of subjectivity that it creates, might serve as a potent symbol of a spatialized moral ordering. As Walkowitz (1992) observes in her consideration of the "imagined divide" between spaces of prosperity and destitution in Victorian London, even if a low-other of society (typified by its "foul practices") is repudiated by the "top," the underclass nevertheless becomes marked by a "heightened symbolic importance" in the imagined universe of the privileged. As Stallybrass and White (1986) observe:

> what is socially peripheral is so frequently symbolically central... the low-Other [and the spaces it occupies] is despised at the level of political organization and social being whilst it is instrumentally constitutive of the shared imaginary repertoire of the dominant culture. (quoted in Walkowitz 1992: 20)

Put differently, the space of chaos serves as an important symbol for the space of order. It provides the vital backdrop against which the legitimacy of the ordered space is established. The conflation of poverty with deviance, impurity with criminality, serves the interests of a spatial and moral ordering which naturalizes destitution as the outcome of personal inadequacy or tragedy and obscures the role of interlocking structural forces of domination. In such constructions, spaces of poverty and marginalization become mapped as spaces of degeneracy.

Dangerous Illusions

Press narratives which produce the Downtown Eastside as a space of chaos have potent symbolic and material effects. In the first place, narratives that privilege an omnipresent foulness and a constant physical danger stigmatize the people who live and work in the neighbourhood and conflate the physical and economic deterioration of the area with the criminal practices they are presumed to reproduce; they effect a "pathologization of the entire neighbourhood." As I argue above, this "responsibilization" has had the important effect of obscuring the key ways that movements of capital have operated to concentrate certain people in certain places. At the same time, policing patterns and state strategies of eviction have operated to concentrate the visible manifestations of a criminality (generally too disempowered to be practiced indoors) in these same spaces.

It is not merely the symbolic cost of this stigmatization that residents of the neighbourhood have been forced to contend with, however. The "chaos" narratives also reproduce and consolidate the view that the neighbourhood has been effectively stolen from its legitimate users, a move that creates a pretext for a "clean-up" of the neighbourhood. Such an eventuality is already being stimulated by the neighbourhood's status as one of the last spaces not yet defined by strategies of capital accumulation on Vancouver's downtown peninsula. A number of factors make widespread gentrification all but inevitable. First, since the 1980s, governments have moved away from reliance on the province's "productive" industrial sector in favour of an economy which privileges the service and hospitality industries, real estate and construction; the state has placed a new emphasis on property development as a means of attracting international capital (Smith and Derksen 2002). Also, as I argue in Chapter Two, a succession of provincial governments have showed a marked hostility towards the poor. Neoliberal retrenchments of social guarantees are but one aspect of the state's decreasing interest in addressing issues of social dislocation. Lastly, the pressures of hosting the 2010 Winter Olympics provided authorities with a pretext to remove "graphic" city enclaves before international visitors and media descended upon the city, accelerating these other factors. The largest single string of Downtown Eastside sro evictions (some 500–850 hotel tenants lost accommodations) occurred in the lead-up to Vancouver's hosting of Expo 86 (Blomely 2004). In spite of early suggestions that the Olympics would actually facilitate broad new investments in affordable housing, little has materialized. In 2008 alone, five low-cost rental buildings issued eviction notices or closed and an additional 180 units of affordable housing were lost. Downtown Eastside housing activists estimate that since the Olympic bid was first secured, roughly 1,800 units of market housing and condos have been built in the neighbourhood while roughly 1,300 units of low-income housing have been lost (Mate 2010). Yet, importantly, narratives that stigmatize the neighbourhood's population play a central role in legitimating this likely takeover. "Drugs and miscreants" are produced as that which stands in the way of a "shining future," as Sommers and Blomley (2002: 52) put it. The symbolic mapping of the Downtown Eastside as a space of "chaos" thus signals a potent danger to those who would be displaced if the neighbourhood were to be thoroughly conquered by a new class of pioneering settlers. Importantly, the neighbourhood has had a long history of resisting such violence and there is reason to expect that no wholesale displacement could occur without a fight. The Olympic Tent Village — a vacant lot turned campsite for homeless people that remained intact for the duration of the Games and acted a means of drawing attention to Vancouver's housing crisis — is a potent reminder of this political vitality.

Beyond the Benevolence of the State

I hope, by now, to have demonstrated that the coverage privileges a series of definitions that inadequately consider the extent and nature of the multiple forms of violence that have contributed to Vancouver's crisis of missing and murdered women. I have tried to demonstrate that these three newspapers have fundamentally failed their readership by mischaracterizing and misdiagnosing "the problem" itself. By asking an inadequate series of questions they came up with an inadequate series of answers. But I think it is important to ask whether this inadequacy really matters. Do the problematic narratives privileged by the coverage have a tangible political cost? I think that they certainly do. Crises of this magnitude — particularly if they are able to generate sweeping media interest, as this one did — can have far-reaching pedagogical implications. This series of tragic events offered, I think, a rare and vital opportunity to inform particular publics about the existence and persistence of certain core modes of subjugation which, in spite of their prevalence, are not always visible to mainstream Canadian society.

By asking tough questions about the striking over-representation of Aboriginal peoples in the grim list of missing and murdered women, for example, journalists might have provoked a wider conversation and a greater awareness about the ongoing effects of colonial violence in this country. By vigorously interrogating the efficacy of the criminalization of prostitution, journalists might have engendered a genuinely public debate about their desirability. By demonstrating the human cost of the ruggedly individualistic politics of neoliberalism, public consent for its particular brand of radicalism might have been further called into question. By looking beyond the lurid displays of visible criminality so easily observed in the Downtown Eastside, journalists might have provided opportunities to re-imagine the neighbourhood as more than a site of concentrated deviance or a *terra nullius* ideal for a pioneering new wave of settlement.

Unfortunately, none of these key pedagogical opportunities were seized. On the contrary, the core explanations that emerge from the coverage lend themselves to a series of problematic assumptions about the essential nature of Canadian society. Disappointingly, not one of the newspapers offers more than a meager challenge to the view that Canada was and remains an essentially tolerant, egalitarian and prevailingly decent society, in spite of the glaring evidence to the contrary that these grim events provide. It is moments like these — when our collective failures are so powerfully on display — that our media institutions are most important.

For me, it is precisely their failure to exploit these ripe pedagogical conditions that makes the coverage so treasonous and unforgiveable.

More than forty years ago, in his celebrated volume *The Structure of Scientific Revolutions* (1962), Thomas Kuhn argued that revolutionary scientific discoveries occur when the underlying assumptions of a particular scientific paradigm begin to be called into question. It is precisely in these fertile moments that "normal science" (or business as usual) is revealed to be untenable and new ways of thinking about problems begin to emerge. It seems to me that the wider conversation provoked by the proceedings against Pickton might well have been the starting point for a kind of Kuhnian revolution of our own. If we had been given the tools necessary to evaluate the violence and subjugation at the very heart of our political paradigm, then the underlying assumptions — that precarious scaffolding that holds our sharply stratified collectivity in place — might well have been challenged in new ways. The "normal science" thinking that has allowed us to rationalize and sidestep what is really at the core of this crisis might finally have been revealed for what it is. Tragically, though, the prevailing definitions that the coverage provides fit squarely within established thinking. Our Kuhnian moment, it seems, has been thrown to the dogs.

I want to be clear that I am under no illusions about what we should expect from our media institutions. I have little faith that tangible political gains will be won by demanding that these corporate structures be more expansive in their considerations of this country's foundational social and political problems. As I argue previously — and I hope the preceding pages have demonstrated — media messages are almost by definition conservative. They are structured in a series of institutional practices that do not lend themselves easily to critical engagement; they both assume and reproduce the legitimacy of the status quo, almost without exception. In this country, these problems are exacerbated by a simple dearth of media diversity. So long as our political classes refuse to interrupt the powerful concentrations of symbolic power that are wielded by the few corporate conglomerates that control our domestic mediascapes, there is little hope that mainstream media institutions will be of much help in any struggle to rethink and change how our society is structured.

So where might we turn for inspiration and analysis? If we can't rely on our media institutions to "comfort the afflicted and afflict the comfortable," as they can hardly claim to do any longer, then where can we look for leadership in achieving these twin objectives? I suggest — in direct contradiction of the media narratives that would have us believe that the Downtown Eastside is a place worse than hell — that it is precisely in this neighbourhood that this task might begin. It is, after all, from within these twenty-one city blocks that some of the most effective modes of resistance and impressive political victories have emerged. Consider, for example, the monumental success of InSite, Canada's first safe-injection venue. The facility sits on the 100 block of Hastings Street, just steps from the notorious corner described so viscerally in the pages of all three newspapers. Here, we do not find a place where "hope fades to black," but precisely the opposite. InSite operates as a safe and reliable alternative for intravenous drug users that are not otherwise well connected to health services. It provides the tools and the space for people to use drugs more safely and acts as a referral and information hub for those interested in kicking their addictions. Preliminary results of this project indicate a range of tangible benefits. Substantial reduction of needle-sharing, increased uptake into detoxification programs and an enhanced access to information have coupled with no recorded increase in drug-related crime and no emergence of any new trafficking culture in the area (Urban Health Research Initiative 2009). Most impressively, however, InSite has now supervised more than one million safe injections and with an overdose rate of more than 200 annually, the facility has not recorded a single fatality (Grindlay 2009; Kerr et al. 2006). Despite an initial public hesitancy, recent polling data suggests that an estimated 65 percent of Vancouver residents now support the project (*Vancouver Sun* 2008).

It is important to stress, however, that this notable achievement (and the immunity from Canada's stringent Controlled Substances Act from which it derives its official legitimacy) was not simply handed down as a benevolent gesture by an enlightened state. On the contrary, it is the direct product of a grassroots struggle. To a significant degree, InSite owes its existence to the battles waged by local residents who — against the backdrop of a spiraling HIV outbreak and a record number of overdose fatalities — decided that they were not interested in waiting for the state to make their lives safer. In late 1997, posters appeared in the neighbourhood inviting residents to a "meeting in the park" where a "community approach" to the area's problems would be discussed. This first meeting, attended by about sixty people, inaugurated a process that would see decisive new forms of resistance emerge in the area (Boyd et al. 2009). In contrast to official priorities that were grounded in enforcement and public disturbance reduction, the bottom-up organizing framework that was developed by this new ad hoc committee was driven by a commitment to personal dignity, harm reduction and winning a shared set of basic demands for survival. Records from one of these early meetings articulate this difference:

> We want detox, treatment, showers etc. They ask us what we want with public consultations and we tell them. We never get these. Money instead goes to the service-providing agencies who hire people with university degrees who get $30,000–$40,000. They set you down and tell you "You have a drug problem," and then they have nowhere to send you anyway for detox or a place to live that won't kill you. Service-providing agencies and their staff lack the political will to change things. They are not for us… Why should people be homeless, sick, beat up, etc. because they use drugs? It's not important if people use or not — they deserve to be

> treated compassionately. When wealthy people use drugs, it is private because they are not homeless. (Boyd et al. 2009: 51)

These initial statements capture the spirit of a politics that has had decisive consequences in the neighbourhood. Driven by an analysis of the political inadequacy of service organizations and defining personal dignity as the core value of their efforts, the framework that was established at these early meetings would soon be practicing a new kind of grassroots activism. The formation of the Vancouver Area Network of Drug Users (VANDU), from its beginnings a member-driven advocacy group, was a direct product of these early meetings. The group sought, among other things, to "inform and empower" drug users and ensure that programs and advocacy structures were driven by users themselves (Boyd et al. 2009). Their work (and the work of their allies) operated to fundamentally alter the terms of the public debate about drug control; the movement was so successful, in fact, that by 2001 all three levels of government had agreed in principle to proceed with a safe-injection facility. But when these efforts were stalled, neighbourhood activists refused to wait for official sanction. In the fall of 2001, a number of neighbourhood activists opened a storefront at 327 Carrall Street and began operating it as an unsanctioned safe-injection site (Boyd et al. 2009). While the storefront would become the target of significant police coercion in the coming months, it served as an important symbol of the unwillingness of neighbourhood residents to wait for the state to intervene on their behalf. Their tenacity proved highly effective and was a key factor in pushing the governments to actually act on their promises to proceed with a sanctioned venue.

There are a number of core lessons that can be gleaned from this struggle. It reminds us, in the first place, that truly progressive public policy is almost always the product of social struggle. The political movements that made InSite possible were not simply passive participants in official dialogues about what was to be done with the overdose and HIV crisis in the Downtown Eastside. Through a bottom-up collective process — driven by those who understood the crisis most urgently and immediately — they had already determined what was needed to make drug use safer in the neighbourhood. Without waiting for official approval, they embarked on a process of putting those needed structures in place. The success of the unsanctioned injection site at 327 Carrall Street had vital pedagogical implications. By defying the edicts of the state and taking neighbourhood safety into their own hands, those behind the facility powerfully demonstrated the inadequacy of the state's approach.

The success of the struggle for a safe-injection site in Vancouver teaches us that when we are faced with governments that are clearly not interested in intervening to make the lives of marginalized people less dangerous, we must move forward without them. When state actors demonstrate that they are unwilling to pay the political cost of taking proactive action then we must take that action ourselves. I remain convinced that these forms of direct action (this *propaganda of the deed*) are our most effective weapon against a state whose negligence is camouflaged by uncritical and irresponsible media institutions. But the InSite experience teaches us another lesson too: political victories are always precarious achievements and the hard work of protecting such gains is often as important as the initial struggle. In spite of its wide popular support and the backing of provincial authorities, Vancouver's safe-injection facility is today menaced by the constant threat of political intervention. Stephen Harper's Conservative federal government — animated by an antiquated Reaganite ideology — have embarked on a sustained legal battle to shut the facility down. Not even a recent ruling by the BC Court of Appeal — which determined that InSite, as a healthcare facility, falls under provincial jurisdiction — was able to dampen federal opposition (Hainsworth 2010). Convinced that retribution and incarceration constitute a sound public policy approach to narcotic use (and armed with vapid ideas about "protecting" families), the Harperites have blithely disregarded the swelling body of evidence that suggests safe-injection sites save lives.

Just as activists fighting for a safe-injection site in Vancouver came up against a hesitant and reactionary state at the outset of their struggle, so too have those fighting to make street-level sex work less dangerous. In this country, we are faced with a federal state that is not interested in proactive action on this front. As I discuss in Chapter Two, the federal government concluded an exhaustive review of prostitution-related laws in 2006. In their final report, the majority of the parliamentary committee tasked with undertaking this assessment concluded that the legislative status quo continues to do more harm than good and urged the government to engage in a comprehensive process of law reform that would refocus state action towards the public health aspects of commercial sex and away from the punitive criminalizing that animates the established approach. Members of the governing Conservative party took a hard line in their dissenting addendum to these recommendations. They argued that prostitution is a fundamentally "degrading and dehumanizing act" often perpetuated against "powerless" individuals; they proposed that the most "realistic, compassionate and responsible approach to dealing with prostitution begins by viewing most prostitutes as victims" (House of Commons Subcommittee on Solicitation Laws 2006).

Months later, the prime minister, commenting on the conclusion of the Pickton trial, echoed these sentiments and made it clear that the crisis of missing and murdered women in Vancouver had not convinced him that the criminalization of prostitution could be considered part of the problem. As Prime Minister Harper put it: "I don't think there's a person in this country [who] cannot react with extreme revulsion to [these] events… in terms of legalization I can just tell you that obviously that's something the government doesn't favour. I think it's a separate debate" (*Vancouver Sun* 2007). The prime minister's neat separation of the Vancouver crisis from the state's approach to prostitution demonstrates a clear willingness to ignore at least one aspect of the state's complicity in the violence perpetuated against street-involved women. His position betrays a distinct preference for the preservation of a supposedly moral purity over the tough work of crafting public policy that would make street-level sex work less dangerous. This is not, however, simply a problem of the excesses of moralizing Conservative ideologies. It is important to recall that Liberal governments were faced with the same challenges as they governed from 1993–2007 and, for all their latter-day lip service, offered little in the way of solutions.

So what, then, is to be done? Faced with a government that seems content with business as usual and a national media that has squandered a vital opportunity to interrogate the desirability of that status quo, how can those of us that are interested in change ensure that our demands are taken seriously? It seems to me that the struggle for safe-injection in Vancouver might offer an important blueprint. That struggle was successful, I think, because it fought a battle on two fronts: advocates of safe injection won concessions from the state by waging both a propaganda and guerilla war. On this first front, they successfully demonstrated in a very public way that enforcement practices were not only failing to ensure a broad public safety but also directly contributing to and exacerbating a crisis of overdose deaths. The advocacy work of users themselves, those who understood what was needed most intimately, coupled with the efforts of allies to successfully make the case that radical change was needed. Those interested in making similar claims about street-level sex work can benefit from a similar approach (and to a large degree they already have). Those of us who are interested in advocating for safer sex work must root our claims in the experiences of sex workers themselves. We will need to both support the efforts of worker-driven campaigns and ground our claims in the rich archive of sex-worker testimony that demonstrates what is wrong with the status quo.

The insistence that sex workers themselves be at the heart of any advocacy effort is crucial for at least two reasons. First, it recognizes that sex workers understand the conditions of their own lives in a far more developed way than any outside observer possibly could; it avoids the condescending presumptiveness of those who imagine street-involved women as "dehumanized" and "powerless" victims incapable of comprehending what is in their own best interests. Second, it ensures that political demands are defined by the people that would be affected by their realization. Of course, it is important to recognize that the sex industry is as diverse as any other labour field and there is no universal set of sex-worker demands. That said, even a peripheral scan of the vast archives of contemporary sex-worker testimony that have been complied by a range of researchers and advocacy organizations demonstrate that certain core themes and demands recur repeatedly. The task for non-sex workers that want to contribute to these efforts is to be informed about what street-involved women have repeatedly told us they need — safe working conditions, affordable housing, access to health services and accessible detoxification facilities, for example — and use our own reserves of social and political power to give those demands an additional voice.

Yet, as the struggles for safe-injection have taught us, demands are far more likely to be realized if they are bolstered by concrete political action; here again, we might learn from those who have gone before us. In the same way that drug users frustrated with the negligence of the state did not bother to wait for official sanction and began to deliver needed services by building their own structures of social solidarity, there are significant examples of sex workers coming together to make their work safer. Such guerilla strategies — be they collective work environments, networks that share bad-date lists, or sex worker unions — not only act as critical barriers to violence and insecurity, they can also serve as public symbols of the hollowness of the anxieties that justify prohibition. The establishment of an unsanctioned venue for safer sex work, for example, might be instrumental in quelling public and state anxieties about the consequences of easing the criminal regulation of commercial sex. In the same way that safe-injection in Vancouver has gradually earned the support of an overwhelming majority of local residents, a safer sex venue might also work to acclimatize certain nervous publics to its tolerability.

Short-term harm reduction strategies are desperately needed and deserving of our support, to be sure, but in our efforts to promote them, it is crucial not to lose sight of the real targets. At the core of crises like the one that unfolded in Vancouver are an interlocking series of systems of domination. I hope this book has contributed, however modestly, to the broader effort to inform ourselves not only about the violence which inevitably flows from a political system defined by racism and stratification but also about the ways in which these forms of domination are camouflaged, rationalized, minimized and converted into commonsense.

References

Amnesty International. 2004. *Stolen Sisters: A Human Rights Response to Discrimination and Violence Against Indigenous Women in Canada.* Toronto: Amnesty International.

Armstrong, Jane. 2002a. "The Short Tragic Life of Sereena," *Globe and Mail* February 27.

———. 2002b. "Inquiry into Handling of Disappearances Urged." *Globe and Mail* February 11.

Armstrong, Jane, and Robert Matas. 2007. "More than 'Drug Addicted Prostitutes.'" *Globe and Mail* January 20.

Barman, Jean. 2007. "Erasing Indigenous Indigeneity in Vancouver." *BC Studies* 155 (Autumn): 3–30.

———. 1991. *The West Beyond the West: A History of British Columbia.* Toronto: University of Toronto Press.

Bauman, Zygmunt. 2007. *Liquid Times: Living in an Age of Uncertainty.* Cambridge: Polity Press.

BC Campaign 2000. 2009. *Child Poverty Report Card.* Vancouver: BC Campaign 2000.

Benoit, Cecilia, Dena Carroll, and Munaza Chaudry. 2003. "In Search of a Healing Place: Aboriginal Women in Vancouver's Downtown Eastside." *Social Science and Medicine* 56: 821–33.

Blomley, Nicholas K. 2004. *Unsettling the City: Urban Land and the Politics of Property.* New York: Routledge.

———. 2003. "Law, Property, and the Geography of Violence: The Frontier, the Survey, and the Grid." *Annals of the Association of American Geographers* 93 (1): 121–41.

Bourdieu, Pierre. 1998. "Utopia of Endless Exploitation: The Essence of Neoliberalism." Trans. J Shapiro. *Le Monde Diplomatique* December.

———. 1993. *Cultural Production and the Field of Power.* New York: Columbia University Press.

Boyd, Susan C., Donal MacPherson, and Bud Osborn. 2009. *Raise Shit! Social Action Saving Lives.* Halifax: Fernwood Publishing.

Brock, Deborah. 1998. *Making Work, Making Trouble: Prostitution as a Social Problem.* Toronto: University of Toronto Press.

Brodie, Janine. 1999. "The Politics of Social Policy in the Twenty-First Century." In David Broad and Wayne Antony (eds.), *Citizens or Consumers? Social Policy in a Market Society.* Halifax and Winnipeg: Fernwood Publishing.

Burk, Adrienne. 2006. "In Sight, Out of View: A Tale of Three Monuments." *Antipode* 38 (1): 41–58.

Cameron, Stevie. 2007. *The Pickton File.* Toronto: A.A. Knopf Canada.

Canadian Centre for Justice Statistics. 2004. *Canadian Crime Statistics: 2003.* Ottawa: Statistics Canada.

Canadian Newspaper Association. 2008. *Circulation 2007.* Toronto: Canadian Newspaper Association.

Carlson, Tim. 2006. "Condofest: Tim Carlson Queues Up for a Woodward's Unit." *Vancouver Review* <http://www.vancouverreview.com/past_articles/condofest.htm>.

Carroll, William K. and R. S. Ratner. 2005. "The NDP Regime in British Columbia, 1991–2001: A Post-Mortem." *Canadian Review of Sociology and Anthropology* 42 (2).

———. 1989. "Social Democracy, Neo-Conservatism and Hegemonic Crisis in British

Columbia." *Critical Sociology* 16 (1): 29–53.

Chomsky, Noam, and Edward S. Herman. 1988. *Manufacturing Consent: The Political Economy of the Mass Media*. New York: Pantheon.

Churchill, Ward. 2008. "Healing Begins when the Wounding Stops: Indian Residential Schools and the Prospects for 'Truth and Reconciliation' in Canada." *Briarpatch* (June/July).

City of Vancouver. 2006. *Downtown Eastside Community Monitoring Report 2005/2006*. Vancouver: City of Vancouver.

Cohen, Stanley. 2002. *Folk Devils and Moral Panics: The Creation of the Mods and Rockers*. Third edition. London: Routledge.

Comaroff, Jean. 2007. "Beyond Bare Life: AIDS, (Bio)Politics, and the Neoliberal Order." *Public Culture* 19 (1): 197–219.

Condon, Sean. 2007. No Place for Home. *This Magazine* (March/April): 18–22.

Culhane, Dara. 2003. "Their Spirits Live Within Us: Aboriginal Women in Downtown Eastside Vancouver Emerging into Visibility." *American Indian Quarterly* 2 7(3/4): 593–606.

Currie, Sue. 1995. *Assesing the Violence Against Street Involved Women in the Downtown Eastside/Strathcona: A Needs Assesment*. Victoria: Ministry of Women's Equality/ DTES Youth Activities Society.

De Vries, Maggie. 2003. *Missing Sarah: A Vancouver Woman Remembers Her Vanished Sister*. Toronto: Penguin Canada.

DiManno, Rosie. 2007a. "For Eastside Girls Nothing's Changed." *Toronto Star* January 22.
_____. 2007b. "Lurid Trial Reinforces Stigma." *Toronto Star* January 27.
_____. 2007c. "Women on Streets 'Still Terrified'." *Toronto Star* December 2.

Eagleton, Terry. 1991. *Ideology: An Introduction*. New York: Verso.

Eby, David. 2008. *The Olympics, Housing and Homelessness in Vancouver*. Vancouver: Canadian Centre for Policy Alternatives (B.C. Office).

England, Jennifer. 2004. "Disciplining Subjectivity and Space: Representation, Film and its Material Effects." *Antipode* 36 (2): 295–321.

Ericson, Richard V., Patricia M. Baranek, and Janet B. L. Chan. 1991. *Representing Order: Crime, Law, and Justice in the News Media*. Toronto: University of Toronto Press.
_____. 1987. *Visualizing Deviance: A Study of News Organization*. Toronto: University of Toronto Press.

Eurchuk, Reed. 2007. "The Cultured and the Cool: Art, Culture and the Vancouver Real Estate Market." *Seven Oaks* April 13. <http://www.sevenoaksmag.com/features/ artsandculturecondos.html>.

Farley, Melissa, Jacqueline Lynne, and Ann Cotton. 2005. "Prostitution in Vancouver: Violence and the Colonization of First Nations Women." *Transcultural Psychiatry* 42 (2).

First Nations Leadership Council of British Columbia. 2008. *Long-Term Impacts of Canada's Indian Residential School System*. Vancouver: British Columbia Assembly of First Nations.

Fiske, Jo-Anne. 1995. "Political Status of Native Indian Women: Contradictory Implications of Canadian State Policy." *American Indian Culture and Research Journal* 19 (2): 1–30.

Fong, Petti. 2007. "A Pig Farmer Who Seemed Easy to Ignore." *Toronto Star* December 10.

Foucault, Michel. 1980. *Power/Knowledge: Selected Interviews and Other Writings, 1972–1977*. Colin Gordon, editor. Brighton: Harvester Press.

France, Anatole. 1917. *The Red Lily*. New York: Modern library.

Francis, Daniel. 2006. *Red Light Neon: A History of Vancouver's Sex Trade*. Vancouver: Subway.

Fraser, Nancy. 2003. "From Discipline to Flexibilization? Rereading Foucault in the Shadow of Globalization." *Constellations* 10 (2).

_____ . 1995. "From Redistribution to Recognition? Dilemmas of Justice in a 'Post-Socialist' Age." *New Left Review* I/212: 68–93.

Fraser, Paul. 1985. *Report of the Special Committee on Pornography and Prostitution, Volume 2*. Ottawa: Ministy of Supplies and Services Canada.

Furniss, Elizabeth Mary. 1995. *Victims of Benevolence: The Dark Legacy of the Williams Lake Residential School*. Second edition. Vancouver: Arsenal Pulp Press.

Gannon, Marie. 2005. *General Social Survey on Victimization, Cycle 18: An Overview of Findings*. Ottawa: Statistics Canada.

Gill, Alexandra. 2002. "Prostitutes, Addicts Too Strung to Care." *Globe and Mail* February 9.

Girard, Daniel. 2002a. "All We Can Do Is Keep Waiting." *Toronto Star* February 9.

———. 2002b. "Despair Stalks Hookers on Mean Streets." *Toronto Sta,* February 10.

———. 2002c. "The Little Sister Behind the Statistic." *Toronto Star* February 15.

———. 2002d. "Police Slow to Accept Crime Link." *Toronto Star* February 8.

———. 2002e. "Relatives of Missing Demand Inquiry." *Toronto Star* February 12.

Gitlin, Todd. 2001. *Media Unlimited: How the Torrent of Images and Sounds Overwhelms our Lives*. New York: Metropolitan Books.

Globe and Mail. 2007a. "The Victims." *Globe and Mail* December 10.

———. 2007b. "A Law That Aids Predators." *Globe and Mail* December 6.

———. 2007c. "The Victims: Six Who Were Killed." *Globe and Mail* December 3.

———. 2002. "Asking How 50 Could Just Disappear." *Globe and Mail* February 27.

Government of Canada. 1982. *Canadian Charter of Rights and Freedoms*. Ottawa: Government of Canada.

Greater Vancouver Richmond District. 2008. *Metro Vancouver Homeless Count Figures 2008: Preliminary Numbers 2008*. Vancouver: Greater Vancouver Richmond District.

Greer, Chris, and Yvonne Jewkes. 2005. "Extremes of Otherness: Media Images of Social Exclusion." *Social Justice* 32 (1): 20–31.

Grindlay, Lora. 2009. "Legal Battle over Vancouver's Supervised Injection Site Starts Monday." *The Province* April 27.

Habermas, Jurgen. 1975. *Legitimation Crisis*. Boston: Beacon Press.

Hackett, Robert A., and William K. Carroll. 2006. *Remaking Media: The Struggle to Democratize Public Communication*. New York: Routledge.

Hainsworth, Jeremy. 2010. "Harper Government Can't Accept Insite's Right to Stay Open." *Xtra West* February 10.

Hall, Stuart. 1996. "The Problem of Ideology: Marxism Without Guarantees." In David Morley and Kuan-Hsing Chen (eds.), *Stuart Hall: Critical Dialogues in Cultural Studies*. New York: Routledge.

———. 1983. "The Great Moving Right Show." In Stuart Hall and Martin Jacques (eds.), *The Politics of Thatcherism*. London: Marxism Today.

———. 1981. "The Whites of the Their Eyes: Racist Ideologies and the Media." In George Bridges and Rosalind Brunt (eds.), *Silver Linings: Some Strategies for the Eighties*. London: Lawrence and Wishart.

Hall, Stuart, Charles Critcher, Tony Jefferson, John Clarke, and Brian Robert. 1978. *Policing the Crisis: Mugging, the State, and Law and Order*. London: Macmillan Press.

Hallgrimsdottir, Helga Kristin, Rachel Phillips, and Cecilia Benoit. 2006. "Fallen Women and Rescued Girls: Social Stigma and Media Narratives of the Sex Industry in Victoria, B.C., from 1980 to 2005." *Canadian Review of Sociology and Anthropology* 43 (3).

Harvey, David. 2005. *A Brief History of Neoliberalism*. Oxford: Oxford University Press.

Hasson, Shlomo, and David Ley. 1994. *Neighbourhood Organizations and the Welfare State*. Toronto: University of Toronto Press.

Hawthorne, Tim. 2007. "Still So Many Questions About Lillian O'Dare." *Globe and Mail* December 12.

Henry, Frances, and Carol Tator. 2002. *Discourses of Domination: Racial Bias in the Canadian English Language Press*. Toronto: University of Toronto Press.

Hermida, Alfred. 2008. "Canadians Increasingly Going Online for News." *newslab.Ca*, June 30. <http://www.newslab.ca/?p=56>.

House of Commons Standing Committee on Canadian Heritage. 2003. *Our Cultural Sovereignty: The Second Century of Canadian Broadcasting*. Ottawa: Government of Canada.

House of Commons Subcommittee on Solicitation Laws. 2006. *The Challenge of Change: A Study of Canada's Prostitution Laws; Report of the Subcommittee on Solicitation Laws*. Ottawa: Government of Canada.

_____. 2005a. "Edited Evidence: 16 May, 2005." Ottawa: Government of Canada.

_____. 2005b. "Edited Evidence: 30 May, 2005." Ottawa: Government of Canada.

Hubbard, Philip. 1999. *Sex and the City: Geographies of Prostitution in the Urban West*. Aldershot: Ashgate.

Hudson's Bay Company. 2009. "Our History: Acquisitions; Woodward's Stores Limited." <http://www.hbc.com/hbcheritage/history/acquisitions/retail/woodwards.a>.

Hume, Mark. 2007. "The Downtown Eastside: A Haunting Ground for Many, a Hunting Ground for One; Root Causes Remain the Same." *Globe and Mail* December 10.

Hume, Mark, and Ian Bailey. 2002. "Police Told About Farm Many Times." *National Post* February 9.

Hutchinson, Brian. 2007. "Not Much Has Changed in the Downtown Eastside." *National Post* December 1.

Jiwani, Yasmin. 2006. *Discourses of Denial: Mediations of Race, Gender, and Violence*. Vancouver: UBC Press.

Jiwani, Yasmin, and Mary Lynn Young. 2006. "Missing and Murdered Women: Reproducing Marginality in News Discourse." *Canadian Journal of Communication* 31: 895–917.

Kerr, T., M.W. Tyndall, C. Lai, J.S.G. Montaner, and E. Wood. 2006. "Drug-Related Overdoses Within a Medically Supervised Safer Injection Facility." *International Journal of Drug Policy* 17 (5): 436–41.

Kines, Lindsay. 1998a. "Police Target Big Increase in Missing Women." *Vancouver Sun* July 3.

———. 1998b. "Cases Probed: Vancouver Police Will Review 40 Unsolved Cases Dating from 1971, but They Doubt a Serial Killer Was Involved." *Vancouver Sun* September 18.

Kines, Lindsay, and Lori Culbert. 1999. "3 Officers Join Hunt for Missing Women." *Vancouver Sun* July 14.

Klein, Seth, and Marjorie Griffin Cohen, T. Garner, Iglika Ivanova, Marc Lee, Bruce Wallace, Margot Young. 2008. *A Poverty Reduction Plan for BC*. Vancouver: Canadian Centre for Policy Alternatives BC.

Klein, Seth, and Andrea Smith. 2006. *Budget Savings on the Backs of the Poor: Who Paid the Price for Welfare Benefit Cuts in BC*. Vancouer: Canadian Centre for Policy Alternatives BC.

Kong, Rebecca, and Kathy AuCoin. 2008. *Female Offenders in Canada*. Ottawa: Statistics Canada.

Kuhn, Thomas. 1962. *The Structure of Scientific Revolutions*. Chicago: University of Chicago Press.

Larrain, Jorge. 1996. "Stuart Hall and the Marxist Concept of Ideology." In David Morley and Kuan-Hsing Chen (eds.), *Stuart Hall: Critical Dialogues in Cultural Studies*. New York: Routledge.

Lefebvre, Henri. 1999. *The Production of Space*. Trans. D. Nicholson-Smith. Oxford: Blackwell.

Levitz, Stephanie. 2007. "Lessons from Tragedy: How Vancouver's Missing Women Changed Police." *Canadian Press* January 7. <http://www.missingpeople.net/lessons_from_tragedy.htm>.

Lowman, John. 2004. "Reconvening the Federal Committee on Prostitution Law Reform." *CMAJ* 171 (2): 147–48.

———. 2000. "Violence and the Outlaw Status of (Street) Prostitution in Canada." *Violence Against Women* 6 (9): 987–1011.

_____. 1992a. "Street Prostitution." In Vincent Sacco (ed.), *Deviance: Conformity and Control in Canadian Society*. Prentice Hall.

_____. 1992b. "Street Prostitution Control: Some Canadian Reflections on the Finsbury Park Experience." *British Journal of Criminology* 32 (1): 1–17.

_____. 1986. "Street Prostitution in Vancouver: Notes on the Genesis of a Social Problem." *Canadian Jounal of Criminology* 28 (1): 1–16.

Lyotard, Jean-Francois. 1984. *The Postmodern Condition: A Report on Knowledge*. Translated by Geoff Bennington and Brian Massumi. Minneapolis: University of Minnesota Press.

Mackie, John. 2008. "From Commercial Hub to the Heart of the Downtown Eastside." *Vancouver Sun* November 18.

Mason, Gary. 2007. "Business as Usual in the Wretched District." *Globe and Mail* January 24.

Matas, Robert. 2002a. "B.C. Police Lashed over Probe; Response by Police under Fire." *Globe and Mail* February 9.

———. 2002b. "Sister Was a Prostitute but so Much More." *Globe and Mail* February 27.

Maté, Aaron. 2010. "In the Shadow of the Olympic Flame: A Report from the Downtown Eastside of Vancouver, the Poorest Neighborhood in Canada." *Democracy Now* March 2. <http://www.democracynow.org/2010/3/2/in_the_shadow_of_the_olympic>.

Mawani, Renisa. 2001. "The 'Savage Indian' and the 'Foreign Plague': Mapping Racial Categories and Legal Geographies of Race in British Columbia, 1971–1925." Ph.D Dissertation, University of Toronto.

McBride, Stephen, and Kathleen McNutt. 2007. "Devolution and Neoliberalism in the Canadian Welfare State: Ideology, National and International Conditioning Frameworks, and Policy Change in British Columbia." *Global Social Policy* 7 (2): 177–201.

McCann, Eugene. 2002. "Race, Protest, and Public Space: Contextualizing Lefebvre in the U.S. City." *Antipode* 31 (2): 163–84.

Mead, George Herbert. 1948. *Mind, Self and Society: From the Standpoint of a Social Behaviorist*. Seventh edition. John W. Petras (editor). Chicago: University of Chicago Press.

Mickleburgh, Rob. 2007. "Guilty Verdicts Make for Bittersweet Day." *Globe and Mail* December 10.

Milloy, John Sheridan. 1999. *A National Crime: The Canadian Government and the Residential School System, 1879 to 1986*. Winnipeg: University of Manitoba Press.

Missing Women Task Force. 2007. "Missing Women: Vancouver, British Columbia, Canada." Missing persons poster. Vancouver: Missing Women Task Force, updated January 25.

Morrow, Marina, Olena Hankivsky, and Colleen Varcoe. 2004. "Women and Violence: The Effects of Dismantling the Welfare State." *Critical Social Policy* 24 (3): 358–84.

Murdocca, Carmela. 2009. "From Incarceration to Restoration: National Responsibility, Gender and the Production of Cultural Difference." *Social and Legal Studies* 18: 23–45.

National Post. 2007a. "These Are Our Sisters, Our Mothers, Our Daughters." *National Post* January 23.

———. 2007b. "The Women He Killed." *National Post*, December 10.

Newman, David. 2006. "The Resilience of Territorial Conflict in an Era of Globalization." In Miles Kahler and Barbara F. Walter (eds.), *Territoriality and Conflict in an Era of Globalization*. Cambridge: Cambridge University Press.

Nilsen, Deborah. 1980. "The 'Social Evil': Prostitution in Vancouver, 1900–1920." In B. Latham and C. Lees (eds.), *In Her Own Right: Selected Essays on Women's History in B.C.* Victoria B.C: Camosun College.

O'Neill, Maggie, Rosie Campbell, Philip Hubbard, Jane Pitcher, and Jane Scoular. 2008. "Living with the Other: Street Sex Work, Contingent Communities and Degrees of Tolerance." *Crime Media Culture* 4 (1): 73–93.

Osborn, Bud. 2005. *Signs of the Times*. Vancouver: Anvil Press.

Overholser, Geneva, and Kathleen Hall Jamieson. 2005. *Institutions of American Democracy: The Press*. New York: Oxford University Press.

Palmer, Bryan. 1986. *Solidarity: The Rise and Fall of an Opposition in British Columbia*. Vancouver: New Star Books.

Parenti, Michael. 1993. *Inventing Reality: The Politics of Mass Media*. New York: St. Martin's Press.

Phillips, Robert Anthony. 1999. "Mayor: No Reward in Missing Hookers Case." *apbnews. com*, April 9. <http://www.missingpeople.net/mayor_no_reward-april_9,1999.htm>.

Pitman, Beverly. 2002. "Re-Mediating the Spaces of Reality Television: *America's Most Wanted* and the Case of Vancouver's Missing Women." *Environment and Planning* 34 (1): 167–84.

Pivot Legal Society. 2006. *Beyond Decriminalization: Sex Work, Human Rights and a New Framework for Law Reform*. Abridged wersion. Vancouver: Pivot Legal Society.

———. 2004. *Voices for Dignity: A Call to End the Harms Caused by Canada's Sex Trade Laws*. Abridged. Vancouver: Pivot Legal Society.

Pratt, Geraldine. 2005. "Abandoned Women and Spaces of the Exception." *Antipode* 37 (5): 1052–78.

Punter, John. 2003. *The Vancouver Achievement: Urban Planning and Design*. Vancouver: UBC Press.

Razack, Sherene. 2004. *Dark Threats and White Knights: The Somalia Affair, Peacekeeping, and the New Imperialism*. Toronto: University of Toronto Press.

———. 2002. *Race, Space, and the Law: Unmapping a White Settler*. Toronto: Between the Lines.

Robertson, Leslie. 2007. "Taming Space: Drug Use, HIV, and Homemaking in Downtown Eastside Vancouver." *Gender, Place and Culture* 14 (5): 527–49.

Robertson, Leslie, and Dara Culhane. 2005. *In Plain Sight: Reflections on Life in Downtown*

Eastside Vancouver. Vancouver: Talonbooks.

Royal Commission on Aboriginal Peoples. 1984. *Report of the Royal Commission on Aboriginal Peoples: Volume 4, Gathering Strength*. Ottawa: Government of Canada.

Russell, Ellen, and Mathieu Dufour. 2007. *Alternative Federal Budget, Economic and Fiscal Update: Can Ottawa Afford More Conservative Government Promises?* Ottawa: Canadian Centre for Policy Alternatives.

Sanchez, Lisa E. 2004. "The Global e-Rotic Subject, the Ban, and the Prostitute-Free Zone: Sex Work and the Theory of Differential Exclusion." *Environment and Planning* 22: 861–33.

Sangster, Joan. 2001. *Regulating Girls and Women: Sexuality, Family, and the Law in Ontario, 1920–1960*. New York: Oxford University Press.

Sibley, David. 1995. *Geographies of Exclusion: Society and Difference in the West*. Routledge: New York.

Smith, Heather A. 2003. "Planning, Policy and Polarisation in Vancouver's Downtown Eastside." *Tijdschrift Voor Economische En Social Geografie* 94 (4): 496–509.

Smith, Neil. 1996. *The New Urban Frontier: Gentrification and the Revanchist City*. New York: Routledge.

Smith, Neil, and Jeff Derksen. 2002. "Urban Regeneration: Gentrification as Global Urban Strategy." In Reid Shier (ed.), *Stan Douglas: Every Building on 100 West Hastings*. Vancouver: Contemporary Art Gallery.

Soderlund, Walter C., and Kai Hildebrandt. 2005. *Canadian Newspaper Ownership in the Era of Convergence: Rediscovering Social Responsibility*. Edmonton: University of Alberta Press.

Sommers, Jeff. 1998. "Men at the Margin: Masculinity and Space in Downtown Vancouver, 1950–1986." *Urban Geography* 19 (4): 287–310.

Sommers, Jeff, and Nicholas K. Blomley. 2002. "The Worst Block in Vancouver." In Reid Shier (ed.), *Stan Douglas: Every Building on 100 West Hastings*. Vancouver: Contemporary Art Gallery.

Stall, Bob. 1999a. "Mayor to Propose Skid Row Reward." *The Province*, April 25.

_____ . 1999b. "Mayor to Propose Skid Row Reward: Mayor Backs Reward in Hooker Mystery." *The Province* July 14. <http://www.missingpeople.net/mayor.htm>.

Stallybrass, Peter, and Allon White. 1986. *The Politics and Poetics of Transgression*. Ithaca: Cornell University Press.

Standing Senate Committee on Transport and Communications. 2006. *Final Report on the Canadian News Media*. Ottawa: Government of Canada.

Statistics Canada. 2006. *Violence Against Aboriginal Women*. Ottawa: Statistics Canada. <http://www.statcan.gc.ca/pub/85-570-x/2006001/findings-resultats/4054081-eng.htm>.

_____ . 2005. *General Social Survey, Cycle 18 Overview: Personal Safety and Perceptions of the Criminal Justice System*. Ottawa: Statistics Canada.

_____ . 2001. *Aboriginal Peoples Survey: Community Profiles*. Ottawa: Statistics Canada. <http://www12.statcan.ca/english/profil01aps/highlights.cfm>.

Taras, David. 1990. *The Newsmakers: The Media's Influence on Canadian Politics*. Scarborough: Nelson Canada.

Teotonio, Isabel. 2009. "School Backpack of Missing Teen Mariam Found." *Toronto Star* October 9.

Toronto Star. 2007a. "Measure of Relief in Pickton Verdict." *Toronto Star* December 10.

_____. 2007b. "Sketches of Six Women Whose Lives Were Cut Short." *Toronto Star* December 10.

_____. 2007c. "Silent Accomplice in the Pickton Case." *Toronto Star* December 10.

_____. 2007d. "Victim Impact Statements at Pickton's Sentencing." *Toronto Star* December 12.

Tourism Vancouver. 2008. "Vancouver Neighbourhoods." <http://www.hellobc.com/en-CA/Neighbourhoods.htm>.

Urban Health Research Initiative. 2009. "Findings from the Evaluation of Vancouver's Pilot Medically Supervised Safer Injecting Facility — Insite." Revised edition. Vancouver: BC Centre for Excellence in HIV/AIDS.

Van Brunschot, Erin Gibbs, Rosalind A. Sydie, and Catherine Krull. 1999. "Images of Prostitution: The Prostitute and Print Media." *Women and Criminal Justice* 10 (4).

Van Dijk, Teun. 1993. *Elite Discourse and Racism*. Newbury Park, California: Sage.

_____. 1991. *Racism and the Press*. New York: Routledge.

Vancouver/Richmond Health Board. 1999. *Healing Ways: Aboriginal Health and Service Review*. Vancouver: Vancouver/Richmond Health Board.

Vancouver Sun. 2008. "Two-Thirds Support Safe-Injection Site, Poll Says." *Vancouver Sun* May 30.

_____. 2007. "Harper Defends Prostitution Laws." *Vancouver Sun* January 27.

_____. 2002. "How Lindsay Kines and Sun Reporters Broke Missing Women Story." *Vancouver Sun* November 6.

Walkowitz, Judith R. 1992. *City of Dreadful Delight: Narratives of Sexual Danger in Late-Victorian London*. Chicago: University of Chicago Press.

Wood, Daniel. 2004. "House Rules." *Vancouver Magazine* April.

Zizek, Slavoj. 1994. "The Spectre of Ideology." In Slavoj Zizek (ed.), *Mapping Ideology*. London: Verso.